Irish Chain Quilts

A Workbook of Irish Chains and Related Patterns

by Joyce B. Peaden

Irish Chain Quilts

A Workbook of Irish Chains and Related Patterns

by Joyce B. Peaden

Group vignettes taken at the home of J.M. & Betty Parks
by Glenn Hall, photographer
Set Designs by Dave Turner

Computer Graphics and Select Photography by
Richard N. Peaden

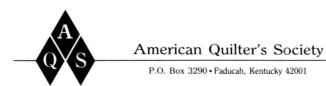

American Quilter's Society

P.O. Box 3290 • Paducah, Kentucky 42001

About The Author

Joyce B. Peaden attended Brigham Young University in Utah with a major of history and English. She went on to receive a degree in history from Utah State Agricultural College, where she met her future husband, Richard. They now have three children, and Richard is a research agronomist for the USDA.

A strong interest in pioneer heritage led her to study and develop talents in the needle arts. In the late 1970's, she intensified her activities in quilting which evolved into teaching classes and workshops locally. Her work included quilt documentation, writing historical articles about quilters and quilting, and a turn at leadership in the Tri-Cities Quilters' Guild.

Joyce made two Irish Chain quilts in 1980, but the intense work on the project did not begin until 1983 when it developed into a fancy to make a quilt in that pattern for every one of her 11 grandchildren.

Special appreciation is extended to my husband, Richard, whose encouragement and assistance made this book a reality.

Thirty-seven years ago, during the first year of our marriage, in Joliet, Montana, I mentioned to my husband that I would borrow some quilt frames from one of the churches, and quilt "that Devil's Claw top" I made at the time of the Battle of Iwo Jima during World War II.

The very next day, his project unbeknownst to me, my husband came home with a full-size easel-type quilting frame he had designed and built that day. (Plans for this frame are illustrated in Section IV-G.)

He taught me to roll the quilt up on the frame to the center two feet, and then to unroll and quilt toward the edges.

He had learned about piecing and quilting as a child in North Carolina, and he had even pieced several blocks with his grandmother, a fact I never knew until 30 years after we were married. His knowledge of cotton material, harmony of colors, patterns and techniques broadened my view. He helped me review my own mathematics and geometry.

And he was patient as my "shop" extended to every room in the house to complete the quilts I made to illustrate the book.

Gratitudes

My mother, Nettie, for her wisdom in teaching her very young daughter the art of sewing.

My father, Angus P. Bennion, for glimpses into history and for the desire to try my own hand at writing.

My grandmother, Mary M. Bjork, who didn't even realize she was teaching her granddaughter to piece quilts.

Dora Smith - Select Artwork.

Sheila Johnson - Stencilling.

Lapin, Exclusive Children's Wear Shop, Pasco, Washington - Silhouettes for Quintyche.

Bertha Curfman, Sunnyside - Quilting: VII-A. Red Flowers and Christmas print, VII-B. Sailboats, VII-E. Old Tulip Applique Medallion, VIII-A. Brown and Gold, VIII-B. Tahoe, and XVI. Irish Ribbons.

Buena Heights Quilters, Buena Heights, WA - Quilting by: Oreen Rank, Helen Fischer, Alice Wagner, Evalyne Vivian, Margaret Loges, Beulah Lee Smith, Virginia Christopher, Charlene Hall, VI-B. Dutch Mill, VI-C. Lambfold, XII. Wine, Lavender, and Fig., and XIV-B. Blue, Brown and White.

Ladies Aid Society, Outlook Church of the Brethren, Outlook, Wa. Quilting by: Stella Lynch, Viola Carley, Tess Korevaar, Rachel Hodge, Bertha Curfman, Barbara Hare, Lucille Gordon, VII-D. Lemon Star, VIII-A. Wine and Gold, VII-F. Covered Bridge Applique Medallion, and XIV-A. Blue, Green and Turquoise.

Quilters Anna Egbert, her daughter Sheila Taylor, and her daughter-in-law Cyrena Egbert of Pocatello, Idaho. IX. Orchid, Rose and Turquoise. Colors by niece Diane Bennion.

Granddaughters Jennefer, colors for VII-A, Red Flowers and Christmas print, and Heather, colors for VII-C, Butterflies. Niece Linda Bennion for colors for VII-F, Covered Bridge Medallion.

Quilting Friends Helen Isaacson, Ruth Schneider, Nora Schneider, Shirley Parker, Jo Yetter, for assistance in quilting XIII-A. Turquoise and White.

The 1878 Domestic Sewing Machine belonged to my grandmother, Matilda P. Bennion, who shared her books and wild flowers with me.

Contents

Introduction

"It is almost as difficult to create a new design as it is to discover a new geometric principle; but another element enters design, and once having learned it as one would geometry there is available, instead of a cold mathematical deduction, a vehicle for the expression of one's personal sense of beauty."*

This Irish Chain Workbook presents the classic forms of the Irish Chain pattern, with some related and several new patterns.

Techniques of construction used herein are in keeping with good sewing principles with emphasis on the best use of the lengthwise grain of the material and the subsequent effective display of both print and plain material.

This method of piecing is precise and efficient; but precludes "free" corner seams that are possible only in hand piecing.

I learned the principles of cutting strips, sewing them together, crosscutting, rearranging and sewing again by observation before I went to grade school. To this day, I envision my grandmother at her sewing machine, as though in a painting, with long strips of cloth feeding into the machine and the sewn unit of strips rumpling on the floor behind the sewing machine, like poured frosting doubling over and over again on itself.

This project began with a Double Nine Patch Crib quilt which I made in 1980 of red polished cotton and the red and white scraps from my daughter's and granddaughter's dresses. I followed notes I had recorded on a recipe card at a county fair 20 years before while viewing a Single Irish Chain quilt. I liked the marvelous simplicity of form and color.

A Double Nine Patch is closely related but is not a true Irish Chain because some of the chains are incomplete.

The Irish Chain seemed the best general pattern for a unique quilt for each of 10 grandchildren.

Our children and their mates are supportive and appreciative. The grandchildren have unhampered enthusiasm. One granddaughter, Jennefer, joined me at the quilting frame at the age of six of her own volition and quilted well from observation.

I am indebted to Tri-City Quilters (Richland, Kennewick, Pasco) and Horizon Quilters Unlimited (Grandview, Prosser, Sunnyside, Mabton in the Yakima Valley), Washington State. My quilting associates have endured with me, and they are special friends.

*Encyclopedia Brittanica, Inc., U.S.A., 1956, Vol. 7, Design, p. 260, (W.E. Cx.).

I.
The Irish Chain Pattern and Color

The origin of the Irish Chain quilt pattern is unknown but is said to have been used in Colonial times. In its simplest form it is a nine-patch block with five pieces of one color and four pieces of a second color, with an alternate block of the second color. Figure I-1.

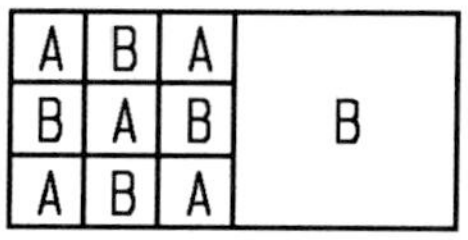

```
A  B  A
B  A  B      B
A  B  A
```

Figure I-1

An evenly scored or divided square alternated with a plain square is a basic pattern or design of ancient civilizations adaptable for wall decoration or floor covering. The arrangement of the colors of the pieces of fabric makes the "Irish Chain" quilt as we know it. As chains are added to make a double, triple or quadruple chain, the respective block in the quilt contains 25, 49, 81 or 121 pieces.

The Irish Chain is a clean-cut, striking pattern. It is consistent in both color and geometrics over its entire plane and is conducive to a restful feeling.

Each quilt requires a minimum of 15 blocks (a composition of 9 blocks will appear as a cross).

The "chain" of square pieces is set corner to corner and may progress diagonally across the quilt or parallel to the edges of the quilt. Figures I-2 and I-3.

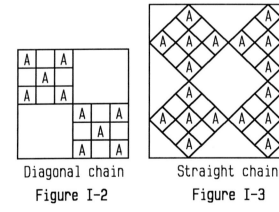

Diagonal chain

Figure I-2

Straight chain

Figure I-3

The chain might be single or in any reasonable multiple. See Figures I-4.1 and 4.2: Comparative Chart - Irish Chains.

Each piece on the chart is given equal space except in Triple Irish III and Triple Irish IV in which each piece is given ⅚ space.

A Single Irish Chain pattern consists of a series of single color chains, each of which is formed by a single row of squares set corner to corner, which in reality appears as a set of diamonds set tip to tip. The individual chains are separated by plain spaces.

A Double Irish Chain pattern consists of a series of two single chains of one color set side by side.

A "Triple Irish Chain" consists of a series of three single chains set side by side. The two outer chains can be a different color than the center chain.

A "Quadruple Irish Chain" consists of a series of four single chains set side by side. The center two chains are identical, and the outer two chains are identical but may be different than the two inner chains.

Alternate pieces form a secondary chain or chains in the Double, Triple, or Quadruple Chain quilts which tend to define the main chain.

The color of the center row should be dominant, whether it is the counting chain or the secondary chain. It is the "A" color in every pattern.

The background can be the same color as one of the alternate (separating) chains, or it can be a third color in the Double Irish Chain, a fourth color in the Triple Irish Chain, or a fifth color in the Quadruple Irish chain.

The background is usually a subdued color. The Extended Double Irish Chain, Plate IX-A, is a notable exception.

The Quadruple Irish Chain can be constructed by adding one additional chain of color onto each side of the chain of Triple II, III or IV, which are shown in Figures I-4.1 and 4.2. There will be six pieces in each corner of the alternate block. Refer to Figure XV-A-1.

An antique example can be seen in *Ladies Circle Patchwork Quilts*, Winter, 1982.

The "chain" might be short or long between crossing points, resulting in small or large plain areas between chains. There are various piecing techniques used to lengthen the chains. I have chosen to call the long or graduated chains "extended"; hence, "Extended Single Irish Chain," etc.

The pieces within the chain are square. Half-squares (triangles) can be used to make pattern "like" an Irish chain, or Irish chain related.

The plain spaces or blocks between the chains are usually embellished with fancy quilting, applique or embroidery. One quilt in this book makes effective use of stencil painting on the plain space. See Plate VII-B.

As a general principle, if the piecing is geometric, the embellishment of the plain spaces should be a curved line design.

Alternate colors may be used for the background or alternate prints of one color may be used for the chain, but the color and pattern must be consistent or the quilt will not appear as a true Irish chain.

COMPARATIVE CHART – IRISH CHAINS

Single Irish Chain

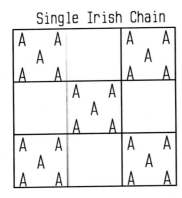

Extended single

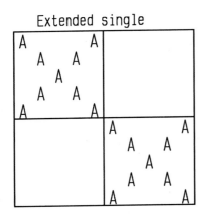

Double

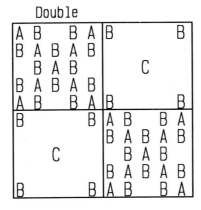

Triple (2 points)

Extended double

Triple II (4 points)

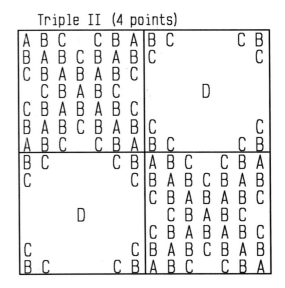

Figure I-4.1

COMPARATIVE CHART – IRISH CHAINS (cont)

Triple III (6 points)

```
A B C         C B A  B C           C B
B A B C     C B A B  C               C
C B A B C B A B C
  C B A B A B C
  C B A B C
  C B A B A B C
C B A B C B A B C
B A B C     C B A B  C               C
A B C         C B A  B C           C B
B C           C B  A B C         C B A
C               C  B A B C     C B A B
                   C B A B C B A B C
                     C B A B A B C
                     C B A B C
                     C B A B A B C
                   C B A B C B A B C
C               C  B A B C     C B A B
B C           C B  A B C         C B A
```

Triple IV (8 points)

```
A B C           C B A  B C             C B
B A B C       C B A B  C                 C
C B A B C   C B A B C
  C B A B C B A B C
    C B A B A B C
    C B A B C
    C B A B A B C
  C B A B C B A B C
C B A B C   C B A B C
B A B C       C B A B  C                 C
A B C           C B A  B C             C B
B C             C B  A B C           C B A
C                 C  B A B C       C B A B
                     C B A B C   C B A B C
                       C B A B C B A B C
                         C B A B A B C
                           C B A B C
                         C B A B A B C
                       C B A B C B A B C
                     C B A B C   C B A B C
C                 C  B A B C       C B A B
B C             C B  A B C           C B A
```

Add one color to convert to quadruple chain.

Figure I-4.2

Color combinations:

Combinations of colors can be visualized by placing the apex (A) of either triangle in Figure I-5 on your choice of color on the color wheel. Appropriate harmonious colors will be found on the other two angles (triad colors).

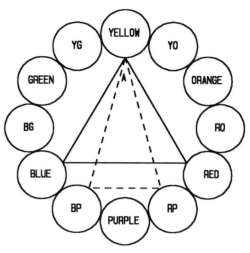

Figure I-5

Complementary colors provide good combinations that are vibrant and mobile. They are found opposite each other on the color wheel.

Adjacent colors (analogous), or a range of adjacent colors, are restful.

Shades and tints of one color (monochromatic) provide dominant-subordinate combinations with intense and subtle values.

One's own personal favorite color, over a neutral color, is a good choice. Try warm jewel colors, such as fuchsia, over black. Set clear primary colors in a field of white. Think of dark nut or bark colors over parchment.

An Irish Chain pattern with narrow borders is very attractive and leaves its expanse free for the impression of travelling, as the eye moves across it. The chain itself is the focal point wherever the eye catches it.

Wide borders may be used to provide a field for fancy quilting or applique when the chain consists of small pieces, or is long enough to maintain its position as the focal point. Borders should have a purpose other than making the quilt the desired size.

Descriptions and block plans shown are also valid for hand-piecing. It is not necessary to cut the strips the same length if individual pieces are to be cut.

Individual motifs may be cut (spot-cut) in one piece of material. Great time can be saved by piecing the rest of the block by the methods shown.

Each quilt can be your own creation, even though you are using a very old pattern. Let your personality be reflected in your choice of colors and prints, embellishments and quilting pattern.

It is suggested that you become thoroughly familiar with Sections II, III and IV before starting individual patterns.

II.
General Instructions for Quilt Planning

A. Pattern Selection

B. Fabric Selection

One hundred percent fine quality cotton is the most tractable material for piecing and certainly the best to use for the method of cutting and piecing described in this book. Other material can be used as skill increases.

Printcloth (in prints or plains) is easier to use than broadcloth.

Printcloth is commonly a muslin material with a printed pattern. It is a square weave material, traditionally 80 square (80 threads to the inch in warp and weft). There are many economy weaves on the market which are more loosely woven, some so loosely that they do not hold their shape and are easily snagged.

Muslin printcloth is commonly called "calico" if printed with a small print of the early American type, or it is just called "print." Muslin is particularly adaptable to quilt making because it is soft and penetrable to the needle for hand sewing and quilting. It is not to be confused with percale, which is a square weave also, but has a finer, tighter weave and a harder finish. Percale is more commonly used for clothing and bedsheets. Bedsheets of this type used for backings are difficult to quilt.

Broadcloth is an undersquare weave, commonly with a thread count of 96 x 54. The "weft" (crossgrain), being the 54 count, has a higher twist to the yarn. The crossgrain reflects the light differently than the long grain.

Plain colors and all-over prints are relatively easy to piece, as opposed to stripes, plaids and ginghams.

The print should have a relationship to the size of the piece. A clear plastic pattern the size of the cut piece, with an opaque material showing the seam allowance, can be placed in various positions over the print being considered to show how it will appear when cut at random, as it is in fast piecing.

The print should be consistent with the long and cross grain of the fabric, otherwise the quilt will have a twisted appearance.

The dye should fit the printed pattern exactly, without overlapping. Some over-dye maybe released in the first washing. It may tint the washwater, but it should not turn it a deep color. It should not run, or stain back into the lighter areas of the fabric.

The fabric should have been stretched squarely, and rolled evenly on the bolt, so that the area along the edges is not pulled awry.

Crease-resistant or permanent press finish is desirable. A good finish is retained after washing. A quality material will have approximately the same body, sheen and resilience after washing as it had before washing.

C. Calculate Materials Needed. Use good steel rulers and sturdy plastic tapes. Seam Allowance: ¼ inch.

The premise of this method of calculating and cutting the material for Irish Chain quilts is based on the idea that quilts constructed properly with the grain of the material will have a "crisp" look, as opposed to a limp or flaccid look. Light will be reflected evenly from the quilt surface. Prints will show to best advantage, without a "sliced" appearance. The quilt will lie flat and stretch evenly on the quilting frame.

The quilts in this book with a straight block set have the lengthwise grain on the length of the quilt, and the crosswise grain on the width of the quilt. The quilts with a diagonal block set have the lengthwise grain from the upper left to the lower right corner.

(Note: Lemon Star patterns radiate from the center of the block, and Log Cabin patterns have the lengthwise grain on the vertical and the horizontal alternately.)

This method shows how a required number of pieces is added together to form a set number of strips. Groups of strips are called "sections." Sections are measured on the material as compactly as possible, just as a tissue pattern for a dress is laid out on material.

All strips (hence all sections) are cut on the lengthwise grain of the material.

Plate II-C-1 shows how a piece of material actually looks when it is cut into sections and laid down on the floor.

Plate II-C-1.

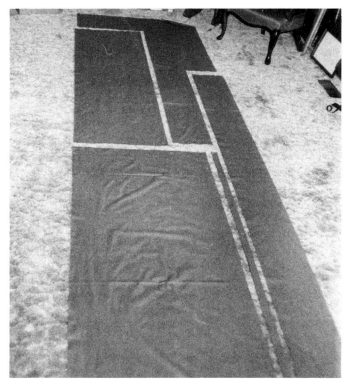

A Cutting Layout Chart is shown with the required width and length of each section for each Irish Chain quilt in this book. All charts assume a 42 inch width washed material.

The charts show the length of strip listed in the text plus leeway.

The charts are drawn to a scale in the vertical dimension which is the width of the material. The horizontal dimension, which is the length of the material, is condensed in order to fit each within the width of the page.

The charts also give yardage figures for purchase which includes an allowance for shrinkage (1 inch per yard) and an allowance for lack of square cut at counter (9 inches on length purchased).

A procedure for deriving these figures is described below:

Borders:

Calculate the amount of material needed for your borders first, inasmuch as they require the greatest unpieced length of material. Allow 3 inches extra to the length of the finished quilt.

Dominant Pieced or Pieced Alternate Blocks:

Calculate the amount of material needed for the strips. Add leeway in comparison to the number of pieces to be cut from the strip and not from the length of the strip itself. For instance, it is wise to add two inches leeway for approximately thirty "cuts," even though no more than ¼ inch should be lost in cutting. A slight slip of the stripper, or similar accident, can occur, though this should be rare.

Determine the length of strip needed for **one** piece, **all** blocks: Multiply the length of the side of the unfinished square piece by the number of pieced blocks of that type in the quilt to determine the length of strip to cut for all blocks in the quilt. There will be as many strips of each color as there are pieces of that color in the block.

Example: Unfinished side of square – 2.5 inches; number of pieced blocks – 32; 5 pieces "A" material and 4 pieces "B" material:
2.5 × 32 = 80 inches of strip are needed.
Add two inches leeway, and enter figure in a cutting layout chart.

Cut 5 strips of "A" material.
Cut 4 strips of "B" material.

Graphic Explanation: Place newspapers around four sides of main pieced block you plan to make in an Irish Chain quilt so that you see only one block.

Place a paper over all of the block except one row.

Now, place index cards around 4 sides of one piece.

Plate II-C-2.

Imagine a strip of material 32 times the length of that one piece which is to be cut apart for 32 blocks.

Now it is logical to see that there will be one strip needed for **each** piece in the block of that color of material. (If there are nine pieces of one color in the block, there will be nine strips of that color.)

All strips of all colors for the pieced block will be the same length.

A strip the length determined will be cut on the lengthwise grain to be sewn to two, four, six or any other number of strips to make the pattern for one row.

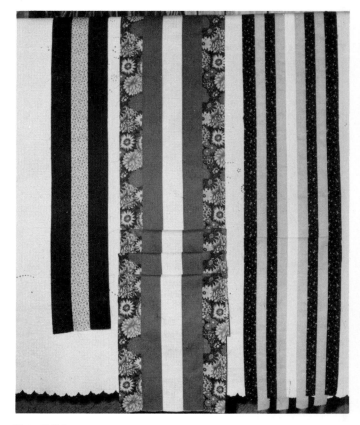

Plate II-C-3.

Note: Strips cut on lengthwise grain sew together on the machine with very little "creeping" that is common with strips cut on the crosswise grain.

There will be exactly as many blocks as needed when the strips are sewn into rows, crosscut and reassembled and sewn into blocks.

Instructions for strips which can best be cut in two lengths to fit available material:

Cut twice as many strips one-half as long. Divide strip length in half. Increase to next multiple of piece and add leeway.

Instructions for strips which are to be crosscut into segments or pieces **before** sewing:

Strips which are to be crosscut into individual pieces **before** sewing, such as segments for sidestrips in the extended Irish Chains, do not have to be cut a specific length.

Figure the total length of strip needed and divide by the total number of pieces replaced, **or** by the number of strips which can be cut in the available material.

Increase to the next multiple of the segment or piece to be cut and add leeway.

Example: Segment for Extended Single Irish Chain, Section VII.

Two strips are required for each pieced block, which are 2.5 inches wide and 6.5 inches long. There are 32 pieced blocks:

$2 \times 6.5 = 13 \times 32 = 416 \div 6 = 69.33$ inches.

Increase to next multiple of 6.5 ($69.33 \div 6.5 = 10.66$. Increase to 11). $11 \times 6.5 = 71.5$.

Cut 6 strips 2.5 by 71.5 inches (remember to add leeway) **or preferably**, cut strips in same length as related section in cutting chart, and retain 1 partial strip extra.

Cut 6 strips 2.5 by 82 inches.

Cut into 6.5 inch segments.

Alternate (or Plain) Blocks:

The ultimate finesse of the quilt is enhanced by having as few seams as possible in the alternate block. However, the block must be balanced. The center will always be a square.

Divide the number of blocks needed by the number which can be cut in the width of material available and increase to the next whole number. Multiply by the length of the side of the unfinished block.

Example: $49 \div 3 = 16\frac{1}{3}$. Increase to 17. There will be 17 blocks in each strip (2 extra).

$17 \times$ unfinished size of block = length of strip needed.

Cut blocks by pulled thread guide, or lay 2 (or 3) strips on top of each other (superimpose) and block to the square carefully. Measure the length of the unfinished side of the block in continuous line with your longest accurate ruler and mark each edge. Place cutting edge on marks, watching grain line for accuracy, and cut.

An exact alternate block serves as a template to the pieced block in assembling and sewing the blocks together for the quilt.

Corner pieces for alternate blocks:

Double, Triple and Quadruple Irish Chains all have a piece (or 3 or 6 pieces) in each corner of the alternate block.

Applique is sometimes used to set the corner; however, piecing will be considered in this text.

Options for providing or setting corners in alternate blocks are:

1. Corner is pieced-in. Section III-C.
2. Corner is set in by strip method. Section III-D.
3. Corner is included in sashing, which also replaces outer row of pieces of pieced block. Section III-E.

Compose Yardage Totals for quilt of a different size:

Table II-C-1. Relation of Piece Size and Number of Pieced Blocks to Length of Strip

Piece Size	No. Pieced Blocks	Length of Strip
1.5	18	27
	32	48
	50	75
1.75	18	31.5
	32	56
	50	87.5
2	18	36
	32	64
	50	100
2.25	18	40.5
	32	72
	50	112.5
2.5	18	45
	32	80
	50	125
2.75	18	49.5
	32	88
	50	137.5
3	18	54
	32	96
	50	150
3.25	18	58.5
	32	104
	50	162.5

The cutting layout will generally remain the same when the number of blocks is increased to make a larger quilt. Copy cutting layout chart for particular quilt you wish to make, and insert new figures. Add the figures together for the sections requiring the longest continuous yardage.

Add the amount allowed for shrinkage and lack of square cut at counter for the purchase of material.

Example: Section V. Single Irish Chain, Twin Size. "B" color material.

58 inches for pieced blocks plus 87 inches for alternate blocks = 145 inches. This is greater than 91 inches for borders plus 39 inches for alternate blocks.

145 plus 4 (shrinkage) plus 9 (lack of square cut) = 158 inches.

$158 \div 36 = 4.39$ yards. Round up to the next nearest $\frac{1}{8}$ yard.

Purchase 4.5 yards of "B" material.

See Table II-C-1: Relation of Piece Size and Number of Pieced Blocks to Length of Strip.

Calculate material for Quilt Backing: Section IV-E.

Calculate material for Diagonal Set Quilts: Section IV-B.

III.
Directions Specific for Irish Chain Quilts

A. Cutting Sequence

Basic Tools: Sharp fabric scissors, rotary cutter and cutting mat, with sand-back aluminum or Acrilic strippers in graduated sizes, Mason's wooden cement float, Tailor's chalk or drawing pencil, silk and safety pins, plastic tape measure and rulers (6 by ½ inch flexible steel ruler, with ¹⁄₁₆ inch markings, and a 24 inch ruler, preferably steel).

Pin a sample of each kind of material to its respective cutting layout plan.

Measure width of each color of material to make sure that it is a full 42 inches wide after shrinkage. Measure length and compare with Cutting Layout Chart. Measure and mark the end of each section with a safety pin.

Note that each section is a set of strips of one width and length for one type of unit in the quilt.

Cut all the sections from "A" material first, then all the sections from "B" material, etc.

Use any of the standard cutting methods for the initial separation of the material into the designated sections, according to the tractability of the material: (1) pulling threads and cutting, (2) measuring and cutting with scissors or rotary cutter.

Accuracy is the prime consideration in cutting both the strips for the pieced blocks **and** the alternate blocks. The alternate block will serve as a sewing template for the completed pieced block.

As each section is cut, place it in a separate plastic bag and label it.

Plate III-A-1.

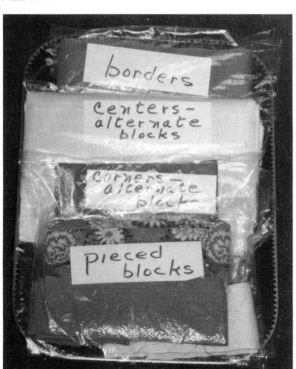

Note: If the material has a nap, establish the top, or "up" end, and keep the "up-end" away from you on the layout table, as it is away from you as you feed it into the sewing machine.

Sequence for each material:
1. Measure and cut backing material, if it is included as part of one of the topping materials. (Selvedges will be removed later as part of the construction process of the backing.)
2. Carefully and evenly remove ⅛ inch selvedge. This can easily be a true thread cut, which will make an accurate starting point.
3. Measure and cut border section, except in rare instances in which combined width of all strips is equal to the material width. Width of borders may need to be adjusted smaller.
4. Measure and cut away section for the longest strips.
5. Measure and cut away sections for strips for alternate blocks, next longest strips, etc.
6. Set aside section for bias binding, if designated. (Refer to Plate II-C-1).

   After each section of material has been separated, bagged and labeled, work with one bag of material at a time, and cut into strips or squares as directed.
7. Strips: Fold each section of material crosswise, as an accordian, and pin at edges. Measure with a long steel ruler, continuously, into the number and width of strips required and mark at each end with pencil. Draw lines and cut with sharp scissors or place stripper and cut with rotary cutter.

   Note: Cutting successive strips depending on stripper alone is not as accurate as above method.

Plate III-A-2.

8. Squares: Measure and cut squares individually or block and superimpose one strip over another and cut.

A wood cement float pressed down tightly over the stripper will increase accuracy, efficiency and safety.

Return strips to individual labeled plastic bags.

B. Sewing Sequence. Seam Allowance: ¼ inch.

Keep the sewing machine clean and oiled. Regulate thread tension. Use a fine machine needle (No. 11) for ordinary cottons. Make about 15 stitches to the inch. Use a narrow, closed presser foot for seams.

A padded table next to the sewing machine is convenient for assembling strips and blocks.

1. Lay out and sew together strips for Row 1 of pieced block. (A row may have 3, 5, 7, 9 or 11 strips in Irish Chains.) Plate III-B-1.

Plate III-B-1.

Put one strip down on the table and lay a second one over it as it falls and pin in place. Make very sure one material does not creep over the other one while sewing. Good material, proper tension and deft handling keep the material feeding evenly into the machine. Sew up to a pin, but not over it. Cotton is adaptable for this type of sewing, but rayon, silk and wool need basting.

2. Continue with strips for Row 2, then Row 3, etc.
3. Press seam allowance of first row to the left, second row to the right, third row to the left, etc. Exceptions are:
   a. Single Irish Chain can be pressed by method above, or, preferably, press first and third row seam allowances outward, and second row seam allowances inward.
   b. Extended Single Irish Chain: Press seam allowances of Rows 1 and 5 inward so that the seam allowances of the center 9-patch unit may be pressed outward.

c. Extended Double Irish Chain: Two seam allowances will face the same direction because the Center Section seam allowance, as it is connected to the sidestrip, is pressed outward in order not to double the seam allowances against themselves. The seam allowance on the left will coordinate with the Row 2 seam allowance but the one on the right will conflict. Open one of the seams and let the seam allowance drape naturally into its pressed position.

d. Lambfold and Quintyche. Note special directions in individual units.

   Learn proper pressing techniques. Press from the right side, holding the material so that you can "tip" the seam allowance to one side with the point of the iron and then press gently over it. Be careful not to press fold of material over the seam. It is often helpful to finger press difficult areas first.

4. Cross-cut each row, using the same width stripper, or the same measure as the width of the strips before sewing. Stack.

Plate III-B-2.

5. Sew Rows 1 and 2 together in chain fashion for an entire set of blocks. Press seam allowance upward.
6. Add Row 3, in chain fashion. Press seam allowance upward. Continue with each row.

Plate III-B-3.

Plate III-B-4.

7. Construct alternate blocks according to specific instructions: (1) piecing-in, Section III-C; (2) strip method, Section III-D; (3) sashing, Section III-E.
8. Sew Pieced and Alternate Blocks together in rows. See Section IV-A, Assembling and Sewing Quilt Blocks into a Whole Quilt.
9. Sew border strips for each side of the quilt together **first**. The narrow strips should be to the inside. Give particular attention to Point 1, above, to prevent extra material in each successive border piece.
10. Sew border sections to quilt, leaving equal amount free at each end.
11. Miter corners. See Section IV-C.
12. Construct backing. See Section IV-E.
13. Assemble quilt sandwich and quilt. See instructions for mounting quilt in floor standing quilting frame, Section IV-F.
14. Bind edges. See instructions for bias binding, Section IV-H.

C. Pieced Corners in Plain Squares.

A plain block with the corners pieced-in provides the best surface for quilting, applique, textile painting or embroidery. A finely woven material is required for piecing in.

Practice piecing-in squares in scrap material first.

Piece all dominant blocks of quilt first. Measure for accuracy. **The alternate block must be keyed to the main block,** otherwise, either the corners will not meet, or the alternate block will balloon out or skimp in.

Making template, cutting and reinforcing:
1. Make a block template from graph paper (large sheet can be obtained from a stationer's) that is the same size as the **unfinished** block of the quilt you are making.
2. With ruler, draw in the seam allowance around the outside edges. Draw in the seam allowance for the attachment of the corners. Figure III-C-1.

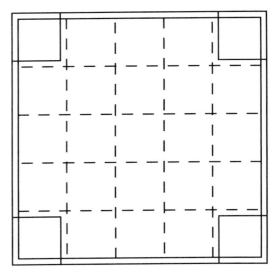

Figure III-C-1

3. Cut corners out. Each cutout will be the size of the **finished** piece you are using.
4. Mark inside corner point on graph paper by making a small hole in that corner, with a large darning needle or other pointed instrument. Figure III-C-2.

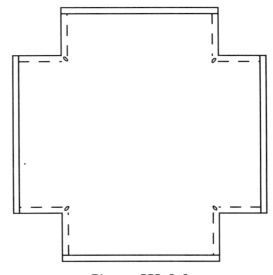

Figure III-C-2

5. Lay this whole block template over plain square block of material, matching all edges and mark inside point of corner square thru small hole and corner edges of template, with a cold water washable pen or tailor tack. Follow alternative (a) or (b) depending on fineness of weave, skill and proposed quilting (if quilt is to be quilted on the diagonal, the line of quilting will go through each corner, reinforcing it).
   a. Mark inside corner point and corner edges. Reinforce inside corner points with fine machine stitching before corner is cut away. Clip to corner point, being sure not to clip the stitching. (Always keep $\frac{1}{32}$ of an inch to the outside of the corner point, for the same

reason that a machined seam needs to be slightly narrower than a hand-sewn seam.)

b. As your skill increases, you will find it unnecessary to mark corner point. Superimpose and hold to the square 4 or 5 blocks. Place paper template. Cut away all corners with super sharp scissors. Establish in your mind the corner point. Clip to corner point (1/32 of an inch short of cornerpoint, as a machined seam needs to be a hair's breadth smaller than 1/4 inch or the measure of a hand-sewn seam).

Sewing:

1. Lay alternate blocks out on table, right side up, lengthwise grain away from you (up-end the material).

2. Lay four squares of "B" material in corners. Be sure to up-end each corner square. Figure III-C-3.

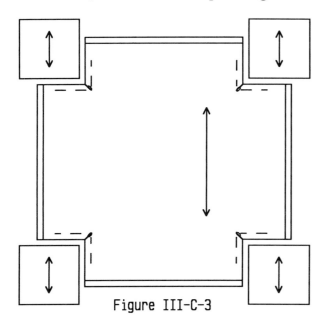

Figure III-C-3

Then turn each corner square to the right of the corner over plain square block (right side together). Figure III-C-4 and Plate III-C-1.

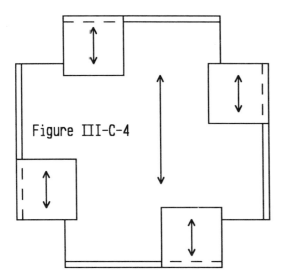

Figure III-C-4

3. Lift each corner and place pin from the whole block side. Turn block over (piece will be underneath).

Place a position pin thru corner of stitching on the plain block and the seam corner point of the small square, line up edges and pin. Stitch to corner, leaving needle in corner stitch. Reach under and pull small corner piece out to match other edge of the cut-away corner, pivoting plain block around the needle. Stitch second edge. Figure III-C-5.

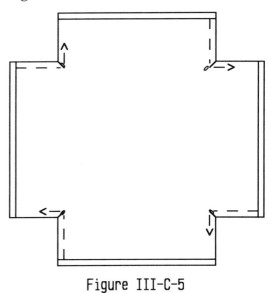

Figure III-C-5

Complete other three corners. Press, with seam allowance toward inside of block.

Up-end all alternate blocks and all corners and complete.

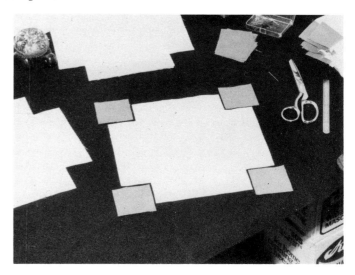

Plate III-C-1.

The Triple Irish Chain has three pieces in each corner of the alternate block.

1. Draw alternate block on graph paper, including outside seam allowance. Mark corner squares. Draw in seam allowances on center section for attachment of corners. Cut marked corner squares

22

out, and mark inner seam point. Figures III-C-6 and III-C-7.

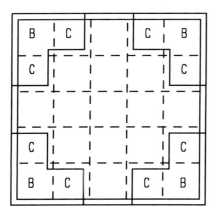

Figure III-C-6

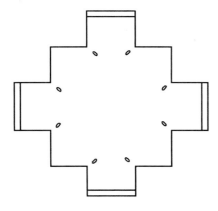

Figure III-C-7

2. Place pattern on fabric alternate blocks. Follow Point 5, a or b, in preceding directions.
3. Lay alternate block, as cut away, in front of you with the long grain up and away from you. Set the first set of corner pieces (you will use the "C" color first) in position with the long grain up. Figure III-C-8.

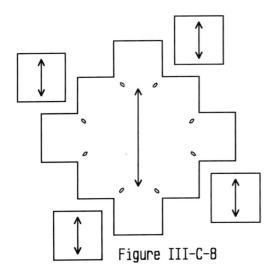

Figure III-C-8

4. Turn four corner pieces over into position, right sides together. Figure III-C-9.

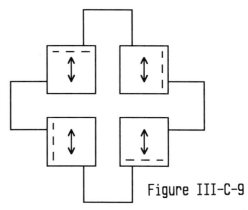

Figure III-C-9

5. Pin from underneath. Turn the alternate block over. Adjust the small piece each time, if necessary, so that the corner point of stay stitching is ¼ inch (slight) from each edge of the single piece.
6. Beginning a scant ¼ inch from edge and fastening threads, sew to corner point (removing pin), stop with needle in material at point, and lift pressure foot. Reach under plain block and pull piece forward to match other edge, pivoting plain block. Finish sewing to ¼ inch (slight) from edge. Open and press with the seam allowance folded toward center. Figure III-C-10.

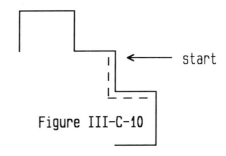

Figure III-C-10

7. Complete this step on all alternate blocks.
8. Repeat process with second set of inside pieces, making sure center and pieces are on same grain. See Figure III-C-11.

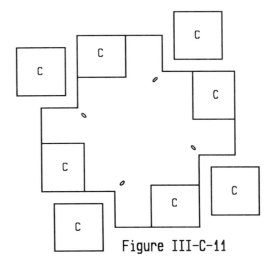

Figure III-C-11

Press. Seam allowance in corner will be free.
9. Repeat with corner piece of "B" color, sewing from edge to edge. Complete this step on all alternate blocks. Press with seam allowance toward center.

D.   Corners in Plain Squares by Strip Method.

This method is the same as the pieced block method wherein a "center" of pieces is made, to which a sidestrip is added and then to which a top and bottom row (or rows) is added. Figure III-D-1.

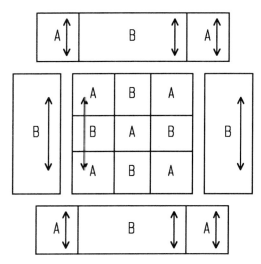

Figure III-D-1

The alternate or plain square block may be divided into sections; (1) the center, which is the equivalent of the finished block less the outside row of pieces plus the seam allowance; (2) the sidestrips, which are the width of the finished piece and the length of the combined replaced pieces, plus seam allowance; and (3) the top and bottom rows, which are the same size but are cut so that the lengthwise grain is across the width of the piece, and consequently on the length of the quilt. Figure III-D-2.

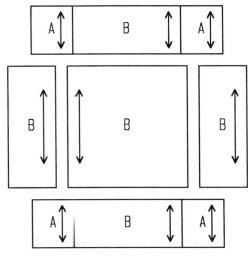

Figure III-D-2

The corner pieces will be figured as strips in the same way as for pieced blocks. They will be sewn to the center

section of the top and bottom row, and then crosscut. Figure III-D-3.

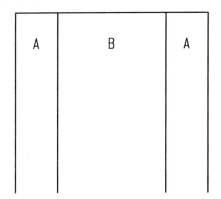

Figure III-D-3

Instructions for calculation:
Center section:
Cut alternate blocks with the dimensions reduced by the width of one piece on each edge. A 10 inch block with 5 pieces in a side would become a 6 inch block, or 6.5 inches with seam allowance.

Sidestrips:
The sidestrips will be figured for each block (pieces replaced plus seam allowance), and then for a total for the entire quilt.

Example: 25 piece block; 32 pieced blocks and 31 alternate blocks; 2 inch finished piece and 2.5 inch unfinished piece.

2 inch finished piece $\times$ 3 pieces per side = 6 inches plus .5 seam allowance = 6.5 inches $\times$ 2 sides = 13 inches $\times$ 31 blocks = 403 inches needed.

Divide by total number of pieces replaced on both sides (6) and increase to next multiple of one sidestrip and add leeway. Cut as many strips as there are pieces replaced, **or** adjust to available material.

403 ÷ 6 = 67.17. (67.17 ÷ 6.5 = 10.33) Increase to 11. (11 $\times$ 6.5 = 71.5).

Cut 6 strips 2.5 by 71.5 inches. Add leeway.

There will be a partial strip extra if it was necessary to increase the length to cut full segments.

Double Irish Chain Alternate Block: The strip can be attached to the center section strip and then crosscut; therefore, the strip should be keyed to the length of the strip for the center section.

Triple Irish Chain Alternate Block: The strip must be cut in segments and a piece attached to each end to complete the sidestrip, before sewing to center section; therefore, the total length of strip can be cut in any lengths desired from available material.

Quadruple Irish Chain Alternate Block: Cut into segments. Attach two pieces to each end to complete sidestrip.

Top and bottom row:
Center section: (2.5 by 6.5) Strips are cut 6.5 inches wide on the lengthwise grain.

Multiply the side of the unfinished square piece by the number of alternate blocks. Cut 2 strips, one for the top row and one for the bottom row.

2.5 × 31 = 77.5. Add leeway.
Cut 2 strips 6.5 by 77.5 inches. Add leeway.
Corner pieces:
Multiply the side of the unfinished piece by the number of alternate blocks. Cut as many strips as there are corner pieces in the block.
2.5 × 31 = 77.5. Add leeway.
Cut 4 strips of chain color.
The Strip Method requires ¼ to 1 yard more material than the pieced-in method, depending on the size of the quilt, because of the extra seams.

E. Irish Chain Continuity by Sashing Method

The sashing and corner system of constructing Irish Chain quilts is a common folk method.

Figure III-E-1 shows a simple division of pieced blocks, alternate blocks, sashing strips and corners for a Single Irish Chain (no example quilt).

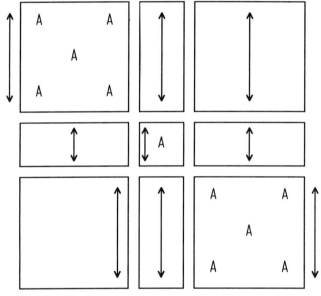

Figure III-E-1

This method is used primarily for Triple and Quadruple Irish Chains.

The pieced block is made with one less multiple of pieces (81 down to 49). Sashing provides the outside row of pieces of the pieced block plus the outside row of the alternate block. The Triple Irish Chain will then have a plain alternate block and the Quadruple Irish Chain will have one piece only in each corner of the alternate block.

An advantage of the sashing method is versatility.

1. The pieced block placed at the edge produces a light appearing quilt with a long inside chain. See Extended Triple Irish Chain III-A, Section XIII.
2. The sashing placed at the edge of the quilt extends the chain one piece beyond that of the regular pieced block.
3. The sashing placed at the edge of a quilt which

is constructed in a reverse set, with the alternate block in all four corners, creates a different look. The Extended Triple Irish Chain IV-B, Section XIV, is an example. This allows for a chain across the corner without which the reverse set would be ineffective.

A disadvantage of the sashing system is a conflict of seam allowances. One of the seams can be opened and allowed to drape back.

Calculation instructions:

Count sashing strips and corners necessary and determine their measurements with seam allowances included.

Each sashing strip for a Triple or Quadruple Irish Chain will include one center and two "sashing corners" (four pieces per sashing corner).

One half of the sashing strip centers are cut on the long grain (parallel to selvedge) of the material and one-half are cut on the crossgrain.

Sashing Center - vertical:
Cut the length of the center on the length of the material.
Multiply the length of the center by the number of vertical sashing strips. Divide by the number of strips which can be cut in available material. Increase to the next multiple of the length of center and add leeway.

Sashing Center - horizontal:
Cut the length of the center on the width of the material.
Multiply the width of the center by the number of horizontal sashing strips. Divide by the number of strips which can be cut in available material. Increase to the next multiple of the width of center and add leeway.

Sashing Corners:
Multiply the length of the side of one unfinished piece by the number of sashing corners of one type.
Cut as many strips as there are pieces of one color in the sashing corner. Repeat for each color and each type.

Corners:
Multiply the length of the side of one unfinished piece by the number of corners for the total strip needed for that one piece for all corners. Cut two strips. The second color will require two strips of the same length.

IV.
Whole Quilt Construction

A. Assembling and Sewing Quilt Blocks into Whole Quilt

Straight set: The chain is diagonal on the quilt. See Figure IV-A-1.

Diagonal set: The chain is vertical and horizontal on the quilt. See Figure IV-A-2.

Straight set of blocks
(P indicates pieced block)

1	P		P		P		P		P
		P		P		P		P	
2	P		P		P		P		P
		P		P		P		P	
3	P		P		P		P		P
		P		P		P		P	
	P		P		P		P		P
		P		P		P		P	
	P		P		P		P		P
		P		P		P		P	
	P		P		P		P		P

Figure IV-A-1

Diagonal set of blocks with optional medallion
(P indicates pieced block)

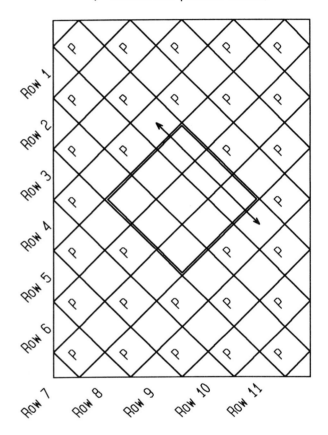

Figure IV-A-2

Note: The number of blocks must always be uneven in both the width and the length for a dominant-alternate setting. There will be a pieced block in each corner. A quilt with pieced blocks in two corners and alternate blocks in two corners appears "unfinished."

Common combinations of blocks in a medium size (9 or 10 inch) are:

Crib - 5 blocks in width and 7 blocks in length (35).
Twin - 7 blocks in width and 9 blocks in length (63).
Full - 9 blocks in width and 11 blocks in length (99).

Each increase in the number of blocks in the same size quilt diminishes the ratio between the width and the length.

A 9 by 11 combination of 10 inch blocks will measure 90 by 110 inches. An 11 by 13 combination of 8 inch blocks will measure 88 by 104.

A diagonal quilt can have either even or uneven numbers of blocks in the width and the length without a medallion. Therefore, a quilt can have five blocks in the width and six blocks in the length.

A diagonal quilt with a medallion must have an uneven number of blocks. Figure IV-A-2, Diagonal Setting of Blocks, shows an uneven number of blocks in width and length to accommodate a medallion.

Example: Diagonal Set Quilt with 59 blocks:
35 dominant blocks
24 alternate blocks
20 edge triangles
4 corner triangles
Diagonal Set with Medallion
1 medallion (9 block size)
30 dominant blocks

20 alternate blocks
20 edge triangles
 4 corner triangles

Diagonal set: The upper, left hand corner will be considered Row 1. Lay the triangles out with the blocks and attach the triangle at the beginning and end of each row as it is sewn. The four corners can be attached last. Refer to Section IV-B.

Diagonal quilts are very beautiful in many forms. They are also more challenging in piecing and quilting, but can be worked very well with extra care.

Lay-out for Straight or Diagonal Set:

Lay the blocks for the whole quilt out on the floor. Keep the lengthwise grain of each pieced and alternate block on the length of the quilt (lower right to upper left of the diagonal set quilt).

Pick up the blocks for Row 1 in order and sew them together. Lay the completed row out on the floor again and check for accuracy of pattern. Row 1 of Diagonal Set quilt will be upper left hand corner.

Complete each row. Press seam allowances of first row left, second row right, etc.

Sew Rows 1 and 2, 3 and 4, and 5, 6 and 7. Join 3 sets of rows. Press row seam allowances up.
Note: Ultimate efficiency.
Straight Set
Example: 32 pieced and 31 alternate blocks.

Twenty-seven sets of A-B blocks (one dominant, one alternate) may be sewn together in chain fashion. Then 9 sets of AB-AB blocks may be sewn together in a chain. Add one set of 2 blocks to each set of 4 blocks, sewing in chain, making 6 blocks in each set. Add a plain block to the end of five rows and a plain block to the beginning of four rows. Figure IV-A-3.

Diagonal Set (no Medallion), with 35 pieced and 24 alternate blocks: 24 sets A-B blocks, 10 sets AB-AB blocks.

B. Calculating and Cutting Edge and Corner Triangles - Diagonal Set Quilts
Edge Triangle:

The finished edge triangle is the same size as half the square block, to which a seam allowance must be added for cutting.

ADD ONE INCH SEAM ALLOWANCE to the finished size of squares which will be used to make triangles for the edge of a quilt. There will be 1/16 of an inch extra at the edge, which will accommodate a variance if the pieced block is slightly larger than the prescribed measure. Figure IV-B-1.

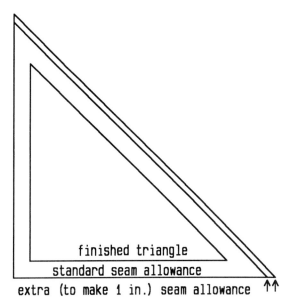

finished triangle
standard seam allowance
extra (to make 1 in.) seam allowance ↑↑

Figure IV-B-1

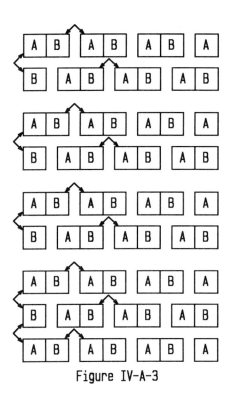

Figure IV-A-3

The long edge of the triangle (the hypotenuse) becomes the edge of the quilt and must be the straight grain of the material. (The equal edge is sewn to the block). Find the measure of the hypotenuse of the unfinished triangle (side squared times 2 and take the square root). Figure IV-B-2.

The best way to prepare four triangles is to cut a square, with the side dimension equal to the long edge (hypotenuse) of the unfinished triangle and then cut it

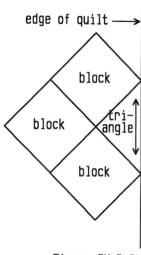

edge of quilt →

block

block

tri-angle

block

Figure IV-B-2

diagonally into four triangles. Each triangle will have the straight grain on the diagonal edge. Divide the number of triangles needed by four to determine the number of squares needed. Use the triangles as "top," "bottom," "left" and "right" as far as possible. Figure IV-B-3.

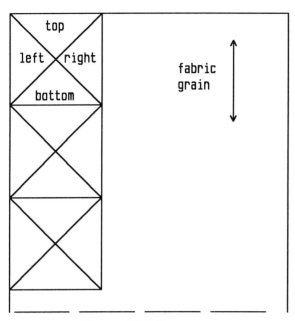

Figure IV-B-3

Note: For nap material such as corduroy, velour, suede or one-way print or uneven weave such as broadcloth: Cut as many squares as there are triangles on one long side.

Example: 20 triangles needed
    10 inch finished block
    10 inch equal side finished triangle
    11 inch equal side unfinished triangle
    15.56 inch hypotenuse of unfinished triangle
    ($11 \times 11 \times 2 = 242$. Take the square root.)

This is 15 $\frac{9}{16}$ inches in fractions or it can be increased to the next ⅛ inch (15 ⅝) for convenience.

Cut 5 - 15 ⅝ inch squares of material and cut each one diagonally into 4 triangles.

Piece the triangle to the square block from the 90 degree corner, **using only the measure of the edge** of the pieced block. The extra seam allowance and the increase to the next ⅛ inch give a wide seam allowance (about ⅜ inch) on the outside edge. A little extra can be trimmed away, whereas a skimpy piece distorts the quilt.

Pin carefully or baste to the pieced block because the isosceles edges are on the bias. Trim seam.

Corner Triangles: 4 triangles needed

The finished corner triangle is the same as one-fourth the finished square block, to which a seam allowance must be added.

The isosceles (equal) edges **must be** on the straight grain of the material to form the corner of the quilt. The long edge (hypotenuse) is sewn to the block. Figure IV-B-4.

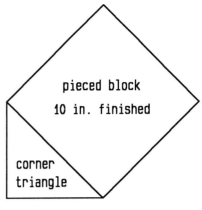

Figure IV-B-4

Calculate the measure of the isosceles edges of the corner triangle if the diagonal (hypotenuse) is known, and add seam allowance.
Example:
    10 inch finished block
    10 inch finished long side (hypotenuse) of triangle
    7.07 Equal Edge of triangle: ($10 \times 10 \div 2 = 50$. Take the square root.)
    $7.07 + 1 = 8.07$ inches with edge triangle seam allowance (Increase to 8.25).
    Cut $2 - 8\frac{1}{4}$ inch squares to be cut into 2 triangles each for corners.

C. Mitered Corners
Fold seam allowances toward border and finger press in corner section.

Trim each border to the square. (Alternately lay each border on top and trim underneath border.) Figures IV-C-1 and 2.

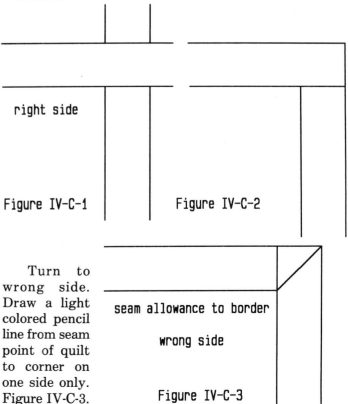

right side

Figure IV-C-1

Figure IV-C-2

Turn to wrong side. Draw a light colored pencil line from seam point of quilt to corner on one side only. Figure IV-C-3.

seam allowance to border

wrong side

Figure IV-C-3

Fold quilt diagonally and turn corners of borders right sides to each other. Baste on line. (Do not press seam line in.)

Machine Stitch. (Use open presser foot.)

Trim ¼ inch out away from seam. Figure IV-C-4.

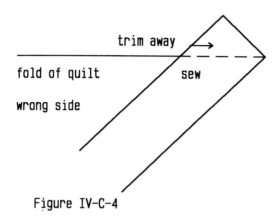

Figure IV-C-4

Open out quilt. Finger press seam open (or to one side as preferred) and stay stitch corner ¼ inch from edge. Press carefully.

D. Directions for Two-Triangle Squares

This is the "tandem" method innovated by Barbara Johannah, *The Quick Quiltmaking Handbook*, with directions added to create two-triangle squares with the lengthwise grain on both halves of the square, and with directions for making the triangle squares with the use of a stencil or perforated pattern.

A quilt pattern may require (1) all right-hand triangles, (2) all left-hand triangles, or (3) a combination of left and right-hand triangles. A two-triangle square cannot be turned sideways without losing the grain consistency.

Note: This is very important with broadcloth, all nap material, stripes and one-way prints. This is not necessarily essential in the use of square cloth, small prints and no-nap material. It is less important in the use of very small pieces over large pieces. Keep the lengthwise grain correct on the dark or dominant material in all instances.

A diagonal line from the upper left corner of the square is a left-hand two-triangle square and a diagonal line from the upper right corner is a right-hand two-triangle square.

Make a tagboard stencil the required size for the two-triangle-squares, for any number of squares desired. The side of the square to be made into two triangles (the unfinished square) will be ⅞ inch longer than the side of the finished two-triangle square, if ¼ inch seams are to be used. Mathematically it is a fraction less than ⅞ inch, but this figure works well.

Rule in the squares and triangles. Mark the **top** of the stencil. Figure IV-D-1.

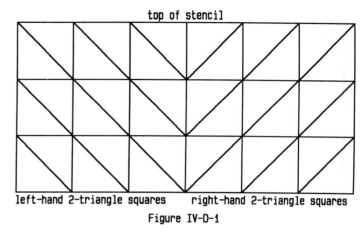

top of stencil

left-hand 2-triangle squares   right-hand 2-triangle squares

Figure IV-D-1

Cut narrow slits in the stencil with an Exacto knife at each inside intersection of vertical and horizontal lines, making a cross. A small slit is needed at the edge of the material, as illustrated. (Slits midway between intersection of lines are optional depending on size of square and confidence of maker.)

Now cut slits a scant ¼ inch away from each side of the diagonal line. (Do not cut slits in the diagonal line.) A scant ¼ inch is used for this, as well as for all machine piecing, inasmuch as a machine-sewn seam is tighter than a hand-sewn seam and a hair's breath of material (1/32 inch) is required to turn from the seam and lie flat. Critical accuracy is required. One square only of the stencil is shown in Figure IV-D-2.

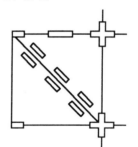

Note: Width of slits is exaggerated in the illustration.

Figure IV-D-2

Lay the stencil with the **top** on the lengthwise grain of the **underside** of the lighter color of material to be used. Cut required piece away from body of material, being very sure it is the exact size of the stencil and each edge is on the straight thread of the material. Mark in the slits with a No. 3 pencil. Figure IV-D-3.

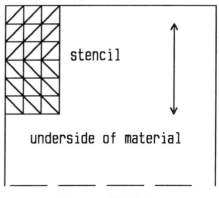

stencil

underside of material

Figure IV-D-3

Place the marked lighter color material, right sides together, over the darker color material, with the **top** on the crosswise grain. Cut away from body of material, making sure it is exact size and on straight thread of material. Figure IV-D-4.

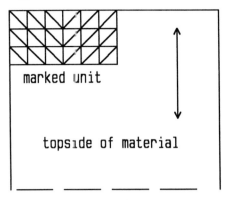

Figure IV-D-4

Place a straight pin in each triangle, as shown by the markings, making sure all edges are even. (If material is slightly awry, it can be pulled gently to straighten the grain.)

Sew on all marked diagonal lines, stopping at the vertical lines, pulling the material past the corner and continuing on the same diagonal line. Cut on all horizontal and vertical lines, separating each square. Figure IV-D-5.

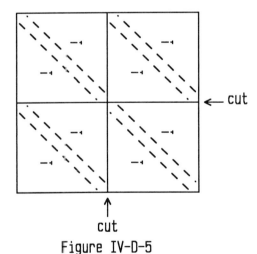

Figure IV-D-5

Cut each square in between diagonal lines. Figure IV-D-6.

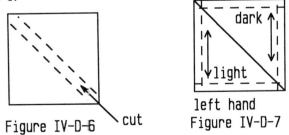

Figure IV-D-6   Figure IV-D-7
left hand

Open out two-triangle square. It will now measure the same as the unfinished square. Note that the lengthwise grain is consistent in both triangles. Figure IV-D-7.

Open seam allowance on very tiny triangles, or press seam allowance to dark side. Finger press seam gently first. The bowl of a teaspoon may be used along with finger pressing. Place the piece on a lightly padded surface and press the seam allowance aside with the teaspoon. Then use steam iron in downward motion only. Do not glide the iron over the fabric.

Compare with square pattern (unfinished piece).

Triangles can be produced accurately with a little practice. If an occasional two-triangle square needs trimming, use a pattern the size of the unfinished square, putting two corners on the seam line.

This method is highly effective with good quality 100% cotton. Results are less accurate with blends.

Note: Parchment paper may be perforated with a needle to produce a pattern for two-triangle squares. Mark all vertical and horizontal lines and the diagonal lines on each side of the center diagonal line. Press pounce powder through the pattern to produce the marking on the material. This is good for a small number of squares in one piece, inasmuch as the pounce powder soon disappears as the material is sewn.

E. Quilt Backing (42 to 45 inch material)

The natural focal point of an unobstructed plane is the center. A plain panel should form the center of the backing of the quilt with part panels of equal width on each side.

Reserve material for backing but do not make the backing until the top is completed. Despite precision methods, final size can vary slightly. Note exceptions for three-length backings below.

Measure finished quilt top. Allow 4 inches extra length and 4 inches extra width.

Determine the number of lengths needed to supply width. Pull threads and trim cut end of material. Cut 2 or 3 lengths as required.

Instructions:

Two-length backing: Figure IV-E-1.

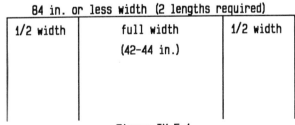

84 in. or less width (2 lengths required)

1/2 width	full width (42-44 in.)	1/2 width

Figure IV-E-1

Quilts which are 42 to 84 inches wide require 2 lengths of 45-inch material (about 42 inches after shrinkage and selvedge removal).

Example: Quilt is 75 by 95 inches.

95 + 4 (leeway) = 99 × 2 = 198

198 + 6 (shrinkage) + 9 (lack of square cut) = 213

213 ÷ 36 = 5.92 yards. Round up to next ⅛ yard.

Purchase 6 yards of material for backing.

Mark right side of material on each length. Also

mark the "up" end, even though the nap may not be apparent.

Fold one length in half lengthwise and press a fold line in exact center.

Lay the two sections of material right sides together, with the nap in the same direction and stitch selvedge edges together, being sure to take a seam that is ½ inch wide. Use pins. Be very careful not to let the material ride over, stretching the top piece.

Cut the selvedge edges away, leaving a ¼ inch seam allowance. Press seam allowance to one side.

Lay tube of material over ironing board and cut down the center of one piece on the pressed fold line. Open.

Note: If the quilt is appreciably narrower than 84 inches, cut to the side of the fold to keep the excess in one piece.

Backing is ready to tack to frame, or to make a quilt sandwich on floor or table.

Three-length backing (quilt top 92 inches wide): Figure IV-E-2.

92 in. width (3 lengths required)

27 in.	full width	27 in.

Figure IV-E-2

Make backing first if a strip on each side of second and third panels is to be used for piecing the top. This excess could measure from 15 to 20 inches in each of outside panels.

Sew all widths together. Trim selvedge. Press seam allowance to outside.

Quilt top 92 inches wide (two-length backing and additional panel from material for top): Figure IV-E-3.

92 in. width (2 lengths plus extra material from top)

7 in.	1/2 width	full width	1/2 width	7 in.

Figure IV-E-3

Sometimes strips can be saved from the yardage for the top of the quilt to add to the regular 2-length backing to make it wide enough for the top. This is more likely if the top is in the range of 84 to 90 inches.

F. Mounting Quilt on Quilting Frame

The quilt should be mounted in such a way that the last point or line of quilting is two inches away from the frame. This is generally accomplished by tacking strips of canvas to the rails of the frame and sewing or pinning the backing of the quilt to the canvas.

The following directions are the "sleeve" method, wherein a folded strip of cloth is sewn to each of the two sides of the quilt to be fastened to the rails, forming a sleeve on each side, into which the rails are slipped.

Cut 4 pieces of muslin from the edge of an old sheet (or similar cloth).

Cut 2 pieces 10 inches wide for the siderails. Make them as long as the width or the length of the quilt (whichever is to be mounted on the siderail).

Cut 2 pieces 2 inches wide for the endrails (the opposite two sides of the quilt).

Assemble quilt sandwich on floor. Backing would ideally be trimmed to the same size as the top; however, it could be left ½ inch larger to allow for some slight error in cutting.

Keep the backing smooth under the batt and top. The top and backing will be equally taut when they are stretched on the frame.

Fold pieces of muslin for the siderails in half lengthwise and lay **on** the quilt, edges together and baste. (Use a backstitch about every two inches.)

Fold pieces of muslin for endrails in half lengthwise, for strength, and baste to opposite two sides.

Baste outward from center vertically, horizontally and diagonally.

Open "sleeves" out from quilt. Slip the siderails into the sleeves. Thumbtack sleeves to siderails every four inches to keep them from slipping when quilt is rolled.

Lay siderails on endrails, forming a rectangle. Square frame and set with bolts (or C clamps).

Roll quilt to inside position (showing about a 2 foot section in the center) in preparation to quilt from center outward.

Note: Roll quilt up to center 2 feet **first** if endrails are short.

Place drapery pins (or any long pin), every 3 inches on end strips of cotton. Lace with sturdy string to tacks or small cuphooks placed on outside edge of end rail.

Quilt from center out to endrail each way, first. This creates what is called a "backbone." Then quilt from the backbone to the siderail, always checking with underneath hand to see that back is smooth from center.

Unthread needle and let ends of threads drop as you reach siderail, picking threads up again as you finish quilting center section and unroll.

As quilting is completed on (wide/long) side of quilt, shift position so that one side is rolled fully to allow other side to open to edge.

Lacing pulls out by removing pins each time quilt is shifted. Lacing is easy to replace when quilt is reset.

G. Plans for an Easel-type Quilting Frame
Refer to Figure IV-G-1 and IV-G-2.

H. Bias Binding
A bias binding is handsome and durable. It outwears a straight grain binding because the edge is across the threads rather than on one straight thread and because it is slightly flexible and the wear is distributed.

G. Plans for Easel-Type Quilt Frame

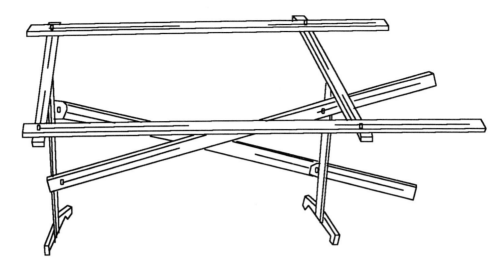

Pictorial view of assembled quilt frame.

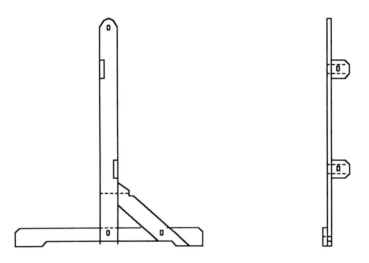

End stand (two required).

Tabs are on opposite edges of the stand to provide matching surfaces for diagonal braces.

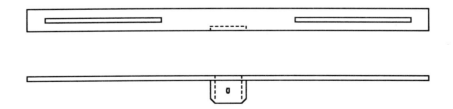

Frame end rail (two required)

Figure IV-G-1.1

Frame side rail (2 required)
Length equal to width of largest quilt to be mounted plus 6".
Slots should be wide enough to allow bolts to slide freely (3/8 in.).

Diagonal brace (2 required)- slots no closer than 3" from each end.
Length equal to frame side rail.

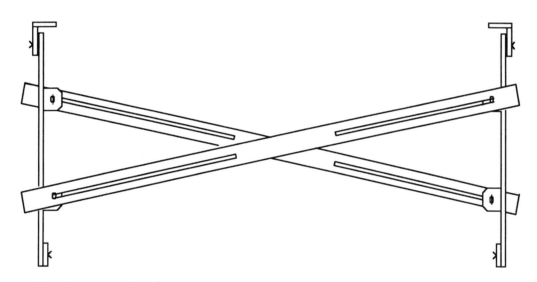

Hardware required
   32 flat washers for 1/4 inch bolts.
   14 - 1/4 x 2" carriage bolts with wing nuts.
   2 - 1/4 x 4" machine bolts with wing nuts (fasten braces to uprights).
   12 no. 8 x 3" flat head wood screws (fasten tabs to stands & rails).

Lumber required
   2 pcs. 1 x 2 1/2 x 30" - stand upright pieces.
   2 pcs. 1 x 2 1/2 x 24" - stand base.
   2 pcs. 1 x 2 1/2 x 12" - braces for stands
   6 pcs. 1 x 2 1/2 x 4 1/2" - tabs for stands and side rails.
   2 pcs 1 x 2 1/2 x 120" - frame side rails.
   2 pcs. 1 x 2 1/2 x 120" - diagonal braces.
   2 pcs. 1 x 2 1/2 x 54" - frame end rails.
   Optional side rails and diagonal braces for small quilts.

Figure IV-G-1.2

A bias binding requires essentially the same amount of material as a straight binding, except for a small triangle at each of two corners of the piece of material used. The loss is insignificant to the whole.

Instructions: Single bias binding.

Note: Double bias bindings are sometimes used. Advantages are that they are completely opaque, give body to the edge, and possibly wear even better. Yet, when the outside layer wears out, the quilt needs a new binding anyway. Counter to these advantages are the facts that they are more difficult to manipulate for fine, narrow bindings and that they require twice as much material.

A ⅜ to ½ inch single layer binding of one of the materials in the quilt is recommended. This requires a binding cut 1½ inches wide.

Dark colors frame a quilt well but sometimes the quilt looks better with a binding the same color as the outside border. Plain colors are generally preferable to prints.

Calculate length of binding needed:

Allow 30 to 50 inches to perimeter of quilt for seam allowances and leeway (the larger amount for a larger quilt and/or a rectangular rather than a square piece for binding).

Example: 360 inches binding needed.

Multiply the width of the binding desired by the length needed for number of square inches needed. Divide by width of material available to find length needed.

1.5 × 360 = 540 square inches ÷ 42 = 12.85 inch length.

This would require too many seams. It would be better to use a square piece of material. Take the square root of 540 inches and round to next higher inch, which would be 24 inches. Purchase 24 inches, or ⅔ of a yard of material.

Fold to a square to establish the bias, and cut the first two strips. Then use the entire width of material (keeping the true basis) to make strips as long as possible. Save corner pieces for another project.

Even very short strips can be used when necessary without seriously affecting the quality. Usually, an additional measure can be added to one of the materials used to piece the quilt and bias strips worked into the general plan.

Cut binding on an exact bias. Do not be tempted by any of the speed methods of producing bias in one continuous piece. They are one space away from a true bias, and tend to give the edge of the quilt a twisted look. Join the bias strips in the conventional way, taking care with nap material that it is in the same direction throughout. Press seams open.

Attach binding to the back of the quilt and finish on the top of the quilt with fine blind or slip-stitches. The pucker created by the fine stitch compliments the quilting. This method was the standard of many fine seamstresses and quiltmakers of bygone days.

Two methods of attaching binding and turning corners will be presented. In either method, prepare quilt and lay binding as follows:

1. Classic preparation of quilt includes a line of quilting ¼ inch from the edge. This insures the edge of the quilt being the same length as the center or inside part of the quilt. Lay binding as it falls on edge of back of quilt, right sides together and baste.

2. Quilt not quilted to edge: Binding must be portioned to the edge of the quilt.

Lay quilt out on flat surface. Fold edge in 10 or so inches and crimp in the extra material evenly throughout the length, so that the edge is no longer than the center part. Lay binding on the edge as it falls (no more, no less) and pin in place.

Baste. Machine stitch. Repeat for each side.

Corner Miter:

Method 1: Continuous binding with folded mitered corner: This is commonly used. It produces a fine square corner.

Attach binding to edge of quilt to the seam point (the seam width from each edge) and fasten thread.

Remove from machine.

Corner: Fold bias binding toward the sewn edge until you can match the binding to the new edge evenly. Baste, and then sew new edge, beginning with the needle in the corner seam point again. Complete all edges, and join binding away from corner in a bias seam. Plate IV-H-1.

Plate IV-H-1.

Turn binding to front of quilt, hand folding a one-direction miter on the back of the quilt, stabilizing with one hand, while folding a second miter on the front of the quilt with the other hand. Pin and slip-stitch.

Method 2. Bias binding with sewn double-mitered corner:

Example: Binding – 1½ inches as cut and ⅜ to ½ inch as finished, with ¼ inch seam allowances.

Prepare a section of bias binding for each edge of the quilt, each 2 inches longer than the measured side.

Pin, then baste bias binding to the edge of the quilt as directed above, leaving a 1 inch tail at each end, and stitching to a point (corner point) ¼ inch from each edge. Sew on machine.

Fold quilt diagonally, right side out, for first corner. Baste bias binding together around the edges of the ends, setting the straight of the material exactly together.

Mark a point (a) a seam allowance from outside edge, and directly across the binding from the corner of the quilt, point (b). Draw a line from (a) on the straight thread of material to point (c) which is in the center of the binding.

Draw line from (b) on straight thread to point (c). Figure IV-H-1.

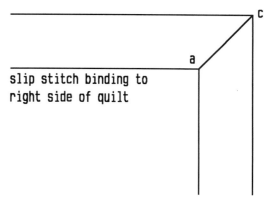

slip stitch binding to right side of quilt

Figure IV-H-2

Gently stuff the corner with a tiny bit of fill if the corner seems too flat.

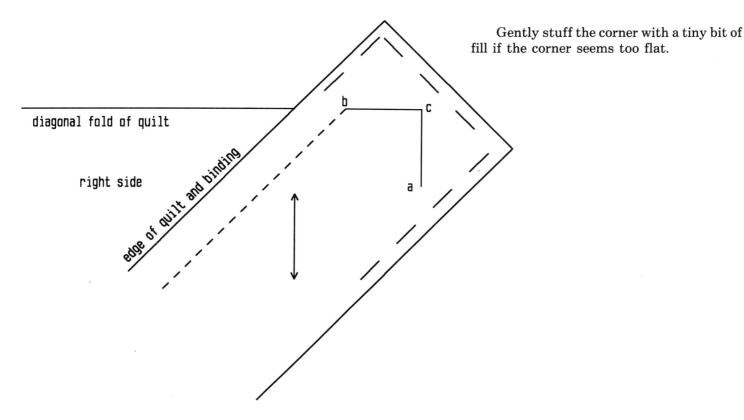

diagonal fold of quilt

right side

edge of quilt and binding

Figure IV-H-1

Sew on line with fine machine stitch from point (a) to (c) to (b). Fasten threads securely.

Trim ¼ inch away from seam and in conventional manner at this point. Finger press (only) seams open, and turn corner.

A double mitered corner is formed and the binding is ready to be stitched in place. Take an extra stitch at the corner to reinforce the machine stitching. Figure IV-H-2.

V.
A. Single Irish Chain

Plate V-A.
Quilted by Author.

The Single Irish Chain in its simplest form is shown in red and white prints.* Figure V-A-1.

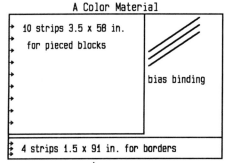

Figure V-A-1

Each pieced block contains:
    5 squares "A" material
    4 squares "B" material
Each alternate block is "B" material.
Figures for a Twin size quilt:
    Size: 7 blocks wide and 9 blocks long
        63 plus 3.5 inch borders = 70 inches
        81 plus 3.5 inch borders = 88 inches
Blocks: Quilt top has 63 blocks with 32 pieced and 31 alternate blocks. Each block is 9 inches square finished and 9.5 inches square unfinished.
    Piece: 3 inches square finished and 3.5 inches square unfinished.
Instructions: Figure V-A-2.

SINGLE IRISH CHAIN

Twin Size 70 x 88 in.

A Color Material

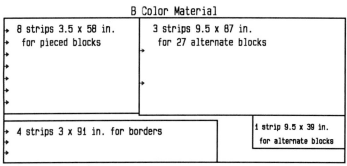

Purchase 2 7/8 yards A material.

B Color Material

Purchase 4 1/2 yards B material.
Figure V-A-2

Add leeway to length of strip listed in text.
Pieced blocks: (32)
    Calculate the length of strip to cut: Multiply the length of the side of the unfinished square piece by the number of pieced blocks in the quilt to determine the length of strip to cut for all blocks. Cut as many strips of each color as there are pieces of that color in one block:
    $3.5 \times 32 = 112$ inches. Cut 5 strips "A" material and 4 strips "B" material, **or preferably**, cut twice as many strips one-half as long, as follows:
        Cut 10 strips 3.5 by 56 inches of "A" material.
        Cut 8 strips 3.5 by 56 inches of "B" material.
    Alternate Blocks: (31) "B" material.
        Cut 3 strips 9.5 by 85.5 inches for 27 alternate blocks.
        Cut 1 strip 9.5 by 38 inches for 4 alternate blocks.
    Borders: Allow 91 inches.
    Binding: "A" material.
    Backing: Purchase 5.5 yards of material.
Figures for Single Irish Chain Double Queen size quilt:
    Size: 9 blocks wide and 11 blocks long
        81 plus 3.5 inch borders = 88 inches
        99 plus 3.5 inch borders = 106 inches
    Blocks: Quilt has 99 blocks, 50 pieced and 49 alternate. Each block is 9 inches square finished and 9.5 inches square unfinished.
    Piece: 3 inches square finished, 3.5 inches unfinished.
Instructions: Figure V-A-3.

SINGLE IRISH CHAIN

Double Queen Size 88 x 106 in.

A Color Material

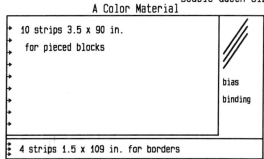

Purchase 3 3/8 yards A material.

B Color Material (top only)

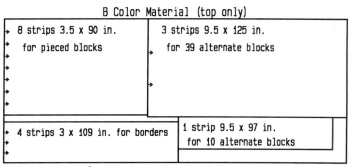

Purchase 6 1/2 yards B material.
Figure V-A-3

* The New Era, The Church of Jesus Christ of Latter-Day Saints, February, 1978, p. 18.

Add leeway to length of strip listed in text.
Pieced blocks (50):

$3.5 \times 50 = 175$ inches. Cut 5 strips of "A" material and 4 strips of "B" material, **or preferably,** cut twice as many strips which are one-half as long, as follows:

Cut 10 strips 3.5 by 87.5 inches of "A" material.

Cut 8 strips 3.5 by 87.5 inches of "B" material.

Alternate Blocks (49): "B" material

Cut 3 strips 9.5 by 123.5 inches for 39 alternate blocks.

Cut 1 strip 9.5 × 95 inches for 10 alternate blocks.

Refer to note for alternate plan.

Borders: Allow 109 inches.

Backing: Purchase 9¾ yards (3 lengths).

Note: Make backing of same material as background and use Alternate "B" Color Material Plan, Figure V-A-4. Refer also to Section IV-E and Figure IV-E-3.

Figures for Single Irish Chain Crib Quilt:

Size: 5 blocks wide and 7 blocks long

45 plus 3 inch borders = 51 inches

63 plus 3 inch borders = 70 inches

Blocks: Quilt top has 35 blocks, 18 pieced and 17 alternate; 9 inches square finished and 9.5 inches square unfinished.

Piece: 3 inches square finished, 3.5 inches square unfinished.

Instructions:

Add leeway to length of strip listed in text.

Pieced Blocks (18):

$3.5 \times 18 = 63$ inches. Cut 5 strips of "A" material and 4 strips of "B" material, **or preferably,** cut twice as many strips which are half as long.

Cut 10 strips 3.5 by 31.5 inches of "A" material.

Cut 8 strips 3.5 by 31.5 inches of "B" material.

Alternate Blocks (17):

Cut 17 — 9.5 inch squares.

Borders: Allow 73 inches.

Binding: "A" material.

Backing: Purchase 4.5 yards or coordinate requirements for the top and backing of the quilt as in Figure V-A-4 (Double Size).

SINGLE IRISH CHAIN

Alternate B Color Material Plan

Double Queen Size 88 x 106 in.

B Color Material with backing included

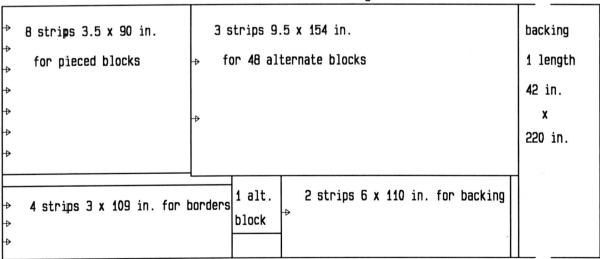

Purchase 13 1/2 yards B color material.

Figure V-A-4

VI.
Single Irish Chain Related Quilts

A. Double Nine-Patch

This pattern, also pictured on page 35 folded on the quilt rack, is often called an Irish Chain, but technically it is not one because some of the chains are incomplete. Figure VI-A-1.

Plate VI-A.
Quilted by Author.

A	B	A			A	B	A	
B	A	B		B	B	A	B	
A	B	A			A	B	A	
			A	B	A			
	B		B	A	B		B	B
			A	B	A			
A	B	A			A	B	A	
B	A	B		B	B	A	B	
A	B	A			A	B	A	

Figure VI-A-1

Each pieced block contains:
   5 pieced squares, each of which contain:
      5 components "A" material
      4 components "B" material
Each alternate block is "B" material.
Figures are shown here for a Crib quilt:
Size: 5 blocks wide and 7 blocks long
   45 × 63 inches (no borders).
Blocks: Quilt top has 35 blocks, with 18 pieced and 17 alternate blocks. Each block is 9 inches square finished and 9.5 inches unfinished.
Piece: 3 inches square finished and 3.5 inches unfinished.
Component (part of a piece): 1 inch finished and 1.5 inches as cut.
   Instructions: Figure VI-A-2.
      Add leeway to length of strip listed in text.
      Pieced Blocks (18): Pieced squares each (5).
Component piece with scraps of "A" material:
      Calculate the length of strip to cut for the

pieced squares of one block. Multiply the length of the unfinished side of the component by the number of components in one square in the block. Cut as many strips of each color as there are components of that color in the square piece:
   1.5 × 5 = 7.5
      Cut 5 strips "A" material.
      Cut 4 strips "B" material.
Component piece with one-type "A" material:
   7.5 × 18 = 135. Cut 5 strips of "A" and 4 strips of "B" material, **or preferably**,
      Cut 25 strips of "A" and 20 strips of "B" material, one-fifth as long (27 inches).
Plain pieces in each block: "B" material
   3.5 × 18 = 63 inches. Cut 4 strips of "B" material, **or preferably**, figure total length of strip needed (252 inches). Divide by 3 (available material) for 84 inches.
   Cut 3 strips 3.5 by 84 inches.
   Cut into individual pieces.
   Alternate blocks (17);
      Cut 3 strips 9.5 by 57 inches.
Binding: "B" material.
Backing: Requires 1 length plus 2 — 2.5 inch strips, or it requires two lengths (purchase 4⅛ yards).

DOUBLE NINE PATCH

Crib Size 45 x 63 in.

A Color Material

```
25 strips
1.5 x 29 in.
for components of
pieced squares of
pieced blocks
```

Purchase 1 1/8 yards A color material.

B Color Material

```
20 strips          3 strips 9.5 x 58 in. for
1.5 x 29 in.       18 alternate blocks (1 extra)
for components of
pieced squares of
pieced blocks                                    bias binding

3 strips 3.5 x 86 in. for plain pieces of pieced blocks
```

Purchase 3 1/4 yards B color material.

Figure VI-A-2

B. Dutch Mill

Plate VI-B.

The Dutch Mill Quilt is easily constructed with efficient principles used for the Single Irish Chain. The pieced block is the same, but the alternate block has a half-square triangle of "A" material in each corner. The corners must meet exactly for the Dutch Mill effect (6).

This would be pieced simply with a 9-patch alternate block with a two-triangle square in each corner; however, it is better to have a plain center. Figure VI-B-1.

A	B	A
B	A	B
A	B	A

Figure VI-B-1

The center might appear to be an octagon. It is not. Sides (1) are the side of the square, and sides (2) are the diagonal of the square (or the hypotenuse of the half square triangle).

Figures for Double Queen size quilt, 88 by 106 inches: Refer to V-A, Figures V-A-3 and V-A-4. Purchase extra "A" color material in same cut for the triangles in the alternate blocks. Hand or machine piece.

Make a template for the alternate block, unfinished, using large sheet accurate graph paper, allowing ¼ inch for seams on the edges and diagonal corners. Cut away corners for hand piecing. Do not

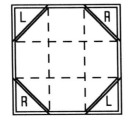

Figure VI-B-2

cut away corners for machine piecing. Figure VI-B-2.

Cut triangles of "A" material as follows:

Cut strips on lengthwise grain. Cut into squares. (You may superimpose 3 or 4 strips to cut squares). Cut diagonally into half-square triangles. Figure VI-B-3.

Figure VI-B-3

Instructions for "A" material for triangles in alternate blocks (49):

Note: Triangle Formula (¼ inch seam allowance on each of two triangles cut from a square): Square plus ⅞ inch. Figure VI-B-4.

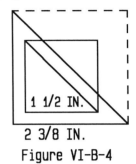

Figure VI-B-4

1. To piece by hand (1⅛ yards extra "A" material):
   Cut 2 squares per block to be cut into 2 triangles each. (Ten 3⅞ strips can be cut in a 42 inch width of material).
   $2 \times 3⅞ (3.875) \times 49 = 379.75$ inches.
   $379.75 \div 10 = 37.98$ inches. Increase to next multiple of 3.875 (38.75) and add leeway.
   Cut strips 40 inches long.
   Cut 5 strips into left triangles and 5 strips into right triangles.
   Piece by hand from seam point to seam point and fasten securely.

2. To piece by machine with second set of triangle squares for another project (2¼ yards extra "A" material):
   a. Cut 4 squares of "A" material per each alternate block.
   b. Mark seam point on alternate block. This can be done by making a needle hole through the template and marking each point onto material of unfinished block (tailor's chalk, soap or tailor tack).
   c. Place 1 square of "A" material on each corner of alternate block, right sides together.
   d. Sew diagonally from edge to edge through seam points.
   e. Sew diagonally ½ inch away toward the corner for a second 2 triangle square.
   f. Cut between the seams.

For each block with a new "A" color corner, there are also 4 – 2 triangle squares in a smaller size for another project.

C. Lambfold

Plate VI-C.

This is a two-color pattern with reverse color alternate blocks. Figure VI-C-1.

```
┌─────────┬─────────┐
│ A  A  A │ B  B  B │
│ A  B  A │ B  A  B │
│ A  A  A │ B  B  B │
└─────────┴─────────┘
```

Figure VI-C-1

Figures are shown here for Twin size quilt;
 Size: 7 blocks wide and 9 blocks long
         63 plus 3.5 inch borders = 70 inches
         81 plus 3.5 inch borders = 88 inches
         Blocks: Quilt top has 63 blocks, with 32 "A" dominant blocks, and 31 "B" dominant blocks. Each block is 9 inches square finished and 9.5 inches square unfinished.
         Piece: 3 inches square finished, 3.5 inches square unfinished.

Instructions: Figure VI-C-2.
 Add leeway to length of strip listed in text.
 Calculate length of strip to cut (it is expedient to cut all strips the same length):
 3.5 × 32 = 112 inches
   Cut 9 strips "A" material
   Cut 9 strips "B" material

 "A" Dominant Block: Press seam allowances of Rows 1 and 3 toward edge, Row 2 toward center.

"B" Dominant Block: Press seam allowances of Rows 1 and 3 toward center, Row 2 toward edge.
 Assemble blocks: press horizontal seam allowances of the dominant block toward the center. Press horizontal seam allowances of the alternate block outward.
 Borders: Allow 92 inches for borders.
 Binding: Purchase extra material of either color.
 Backing: Purchase 5.5 yards of material.

LAMBFOLD

Twin Size 70 x 88 in.
A Color Material

```
┌─────────────────────────────────────────┬──────┐
│ 9 strips 3.5 x 114 in. for pieced blocks │      │
│                                          │      │
│                                          │      │
│                                          │      │
│                                          │      │
│                                          │      │
│                                          │      │
│                                          │      │
├──────────────────────────────────┬───────┤
│ 4 strips 2.5 x 92 in. for borders │ scrap │
└───────────────────────────────────┴───────┘
```

Purchase 3 1/2 yards A material.

B Color Material

```
┌─────────────────────────────────────────────┐
│ 9 strips 3.5 x 114 in. for pieced blocks     │
│                                              │
│                                              │
│                                              │
│                                              │
│                                              │
│                                              │
├──────────────────────────────────────┬───────┤
│ scrap                                 │       │
├──────────────────────────────────────┘       │
│ 4 strips 1.5 x 92 in. for borders            │
└──────────────────────────────────────────────┘
```

Purchase 3 1/2 yards B material.
Figure VI-C-2

D. Quintyche

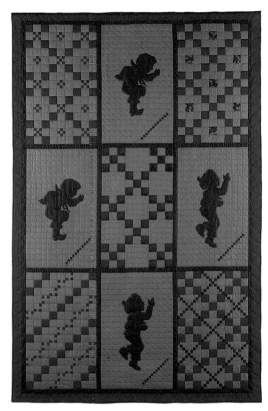

Plate VI-D.
Quilted by Author.

This original quilt is a medley of five patterns, Irish Shadows, Web, Jewels, Stony Paths and Echo. The patterns are interspersed with enlarged "newspaper art" silhouettes. The format of this quilt could be used with any creative ideas for interplay of Irish Chains, and one's own individualistic silhouettes.

Note: Silhouettes are two figures from the newspaper advertisement of the Lapin, Exclusive Children's Wear Shop in Pasco, Washington. No pattern.

The term "tyche" is from a Greek word, meaning an idea that sprang forth. "Quin" means "five," of course, a manner of counting with the five fingers (Rome).

Each pattern could be made into a full size quilt by following the formulas for cutting and piecing material described in this book.

The idea was developed from Robert Louis Stevenson's poem, "My Shadow."

If the Irish Chain pattern really came from Ireland, there should be a derivitive of the pattern that is reminiscent of the countryside of Ireland. The pattern, Irish Stony paths, is my interpretation in cloth of footpaths through rocky terrain, which was suggested by a picture in *The National Geographic* magazine.

Figures for Twin size quilt: 71.25 by 111.75 inches
Size: 3 panels wide by 3 panels long,
   1.25 inch sashing, 4 inch borders
   Panel: 20.25 by 33.75 inches, finished
Blocks: 6.75 inches square finished, and 7.25 inches unfinished. There are eight dominant and seven alternate

blocks in each panel.
   Piece: 2.25 inches square finished and 2.75 inches as cut.
   Component: (part of a piece) .75 inch (Paths, Echo, Web).
Silhouettes Panel:
   Cut 4 units of background material 20.75 by 34.25 inches. (It is wise to allow ½ inch leeway for variance in piecing – 21.25 × 34.75.)
Silhouettes:
   Cut 4 silhouettes of "D" material.
Instructions: Figures VI-D-3.1, 3.2.
   Borders (triple): Allow 75 inches for top and bottom borders and 116 inches for side borders.
   Binding: "D" material or optional. Purchase separately.
   Backing: Purchase 7 yards of material.

Irish Shadows Center Panel

A Log Cabin technique is used to piece the five "chain" pieces of the dominant block. The components of the piece graduate and decrease in size as do shadows.

Panel, Block and Piece Measurements are the same in all five patterns. There are 4 types of pieced blocks (1, 3, 3, 1) and 7 alternate blocks.

Leeway suggested is ¼ inch to a strip. Figures in parenthesis are, first, actual total length of strip needed, and second, total length of strip needed with leeway added.

Type I: 1 block.
   Cut 5 - 1 inch squares of "A" material.
   Cut 5 strips .75 by 2.25 inches of "C" material.
   Cut 5 strips 2 by 4 inches of "D" material (20 - 21.25).
Type II: 3 blocks.
   Cut 5 - 1.75 inch squares of "A" material for each block.
   Cut 5 strips .75 by 3.75 inches of "C" material for each block.
   Cut 5 strips 1.25 by 4.75 inches of "D" material for each block (71.25 - 75).
Type III: 3 blocks.
   Cut 5 - 2 inch squares of "A" material for each block.
   Cut 5 strips .75 by 4.25 inches of "C" material for each block.
   Cut 5 strips 1 by 5 inches of "D" material for each block (75 - 78.75)
Type IV: 1 block.
   Cut 5 - 2.25 inch squares of "A" material.
   Cut 5 strips .75 by 4.75 inches of "C" material.
   Cut 5 strips .75 by 5.25 inches of "D" material (26.25 - 27.5).

Irish Web Upper Left Panel

Instructions: Figures VI-D-3.1, 3.2,
Dominant Block (8):
2.75 × 8 = 22 inches
Cut 4 strips of "A" material and 4 strips of "B" material. Please add leeway.
Center Piece: (Nine components)
1.25 × 8 = 10 inches
Cut 5 strips of "A" material.
Cut 4 strips of "B" material.
Alternate Block (7):
2.75 × 7 = 19.25 inches
Cut 8 strips of "B" material.
Center piece: (Nine components)
1.25 × 7 = 8.75 inches
Cut 4 strips of "A" material.
Cut 5 strips of "B" material.

Irish Jewels Upper Right Panel

An idea of bright drops of color is created by Crazy-Patch facets.
Instructions: Figures VI-D-3.1, 3.2.
Dominant Block (8):
2.75 × 8 = 22 inches (add leeway).
Cut 5 strips "A" material.
Cut 4 strips "B" material.
Alternate Block (7):
Jewel Center:
Cut 48 strips 1.5 by 7 inches from scraps (four colors - 12 strips each.)
Trim (layers of four) to a wedge shape without a point. Figure VI-D-1.

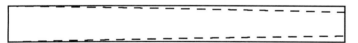

Figure VI-D-1

Piece together in successive color combinations, beginning left edge with wide, narrow, etc. Figure VI-D-2.

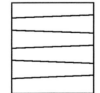

Figure VI-D-2

Cross cut into 8 pieces each (7 required), and assemble.
Make transparent template for unfinished piece (2.75). Adjust over Crazy-patch piece and trim to size.
Background pieces: (7 alternate blocks)
2.75 × 7 = 19.25 (add leeway).
Cut 8 strips of "B" material.

Irish Stony Paths Lower Left Panel

Stony Paths has a diagonal pattern in one direction only.
Instructions: Figures VI-D-3.1, 3.2.
Dominant Block (8):
2.75 × 8 = 22 inches (add leeway)
Cut 3 strips of "A" material.
Cut 6 strips of "B" material.
Press seam allowance of Rows 1 and 3 toward edge, and Row 2 toward center.
Alternate Block (7):
2.75 × 7 = 19.25 inches (add leeway)
Cut 6 strips of "B" material.
Nine-patch: 3 "C" and 6 "B" components each
1.25 × 21 = 26.25 (add leeway)
Cut 3 strips of "C" material.
Cut 6 strips of "B" material.
Sew together 2 sets of strips before crosscutting. Cut remaining 2 strips into squares, and add to set.
Note: There are 11 "up" pieced squares and 10 "down" pieced squares (reversed). If material has a nap or a one way print, the 10 "down" pieced squares must be constructed separately.
Assemble alternate blocks. Three (center blocks) will be reversed. Construct separately if there is a nap.
Press seam allowance of Rows 1 and 3 toward center, and Row 2 toward edge.
Assemble blocks: Press seam allowances of the dominant block toward the center. Press seam allowances of the alternate block outward.

Quintyche - Irish Echo Lower Right Panel

The echo quilt uses the alternate block to repeat, in small pieces and dark color, the Single Irish Chain of the main pieced block.
Instructions: Figures VI-D-3.1, 3.2.
Dominant block (8):
2.75 × 8 = 22 inches (add leeway)
Cut 5 strips of "A" material.
Cut 4 strips of "B" material.
Press seam allowance of Rows 1 and 3 toward edge, and Row 2 toward center.
Alternate block (7) (five pieced and four plain squares)
2.75 × 7 = 19.25 inches (add leeway)
Cut 4 strips of "B" material.
Nine-patch (5 per alternate block): 17 "D" and 28 "B" components)
1.25 × 7 = 8.75 inches
Cut 17 strips "D" material and 28 strips "B" material **or preferably**, make the center Nine-patch separately, and then make the four corner pieces, as follows:
Cut 5 strips of "D" material 8,75 inches long, and 4 strips of "B" material 8.75 inches long for

long for center nine-patch.

That leaves 12 strips of "D" and 24 strips of "B" material. Two strips may be cut in one length for left-hand and right-hand chains. There will be half as many strips.

2 strips $\times$ 8.75 = 17.5 inches (add leeway)

Cut 6 strips of "D" material

Cut 12 strips of "B" material.

Press seam allowance of Rows 1 and 3 toward center, and Row 2 toward edge.

Assemble blocks: Press horizontal seam allowances of the dominant block toward the center. Press horizontal seam allowances of the alternate block outward.

QUINTYCHE

Twin Size 72 x 112 in.

A Color Material

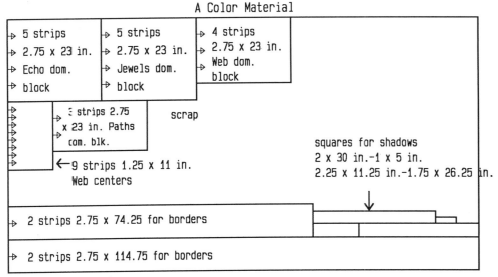

Purchase 3 5/8 yards A color material for unpieced borders or
2 1/2 yards for pieced borders.

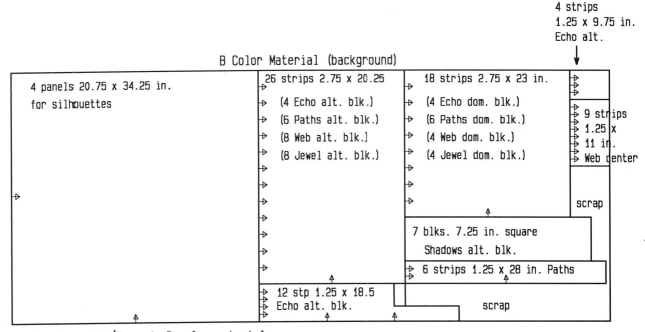

Purchase 5 1/2 yards B color material.

Figure VI-D-3.1

QUINTYCHE

Twin Size 72 x 112 in.

C Color Material

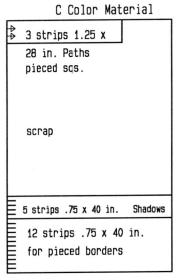

3 strips 1.25 x
28 in. Paths
pieced sqs.

scrap

5 strips .75 x 40 in.   Shadows
12 strips .75 x 40 in.
for pieced borders

Purchase 1 1/2 yards C color material (pieced borders).

D Color Material

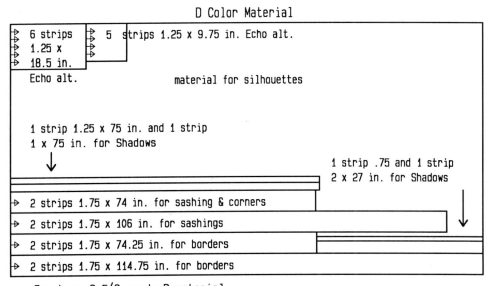

6 strips
1.25 x
18.5 in.
Echo alt.

5 strips 1.25 x 9.75 in. Echo alt.

material for silhouettes

1 strip 1.25 x 75 in. and 1 strip
1 x 75 in. for Shadows

1 strip .75 and 1 strip
2 x 27 in. for Shadows

2 strips 1.75 x 74 in. for sashing & corners
2 strips 1.75 x 106 in. for sashings
2 strips 1.75 x 74.25 in. for borders
2 strips 1.75 x 114.75 in. for borders

Purchase 3 5/8 yards D material.

Figure VI-D-3.2

VII.
Extended Single Irish Chain

A. Red Flowers and Christmas Prints

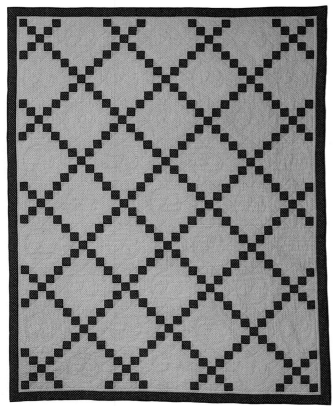

Plate VII-A.

This light, airy looking form of the Single Irish Chain is composed with a 25-piece block, of which 9 pieces form the chain, alternating with a plain block. Figure VII-A-1.

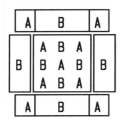

Figure VII-A-1

Each pieced block contains:
    9 squares "A" material
    16 squares "B" material
        Three squares of one color occurring together will be cut as one piece.
Each alternate block is "B" material.
Figures are shown here for Twin Double size quilt:
    Size: 7 blocks wide and 9 blocks long
        70 plus 2.5 inch borders = 75 inches
        90 plus 2.5 inch borders = 95 inches
Blocks: Quilt top has 63 blocks with 32 pieced and 31 alternate blocks. Each block is 10 inches square finished, and 10.5 inches square unfinished.
    Piece: 2 inches square finished, and 2.5 inches square unfinished. Three pieces together are 2 by 6 inches finished and 2.5 by 6.5 inches unfinished.
Instructions: Figure VII-A-2.

EXTENDED SINGLE IRISH CHAIN
Twin Double Size 75 x 95 in.

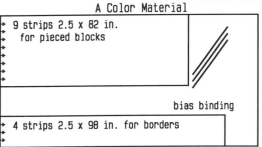

Purchase 3 1/8 yards A color material.

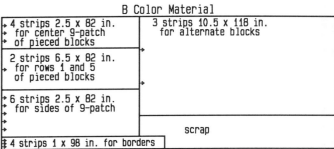

Purchase 6 yards B color material.
Figure VII-A-2

Add leeway to length of strip listed in text.
Pieced blocks (32): Refer to Section III-D.
    The pieced blocks will be constructed in this manner: The nine pieces in the center will be considered as a nine-patch. Sidestrips of "B" material will be sewn to this center nine-patch.
    The top and bottom row will be constructed by sewing 2.5 inch strips of "A" material on each side of a 6.5 inch strip of "B" material and then cutting that unit crosswise into 2.5 inch units.
    Calculate the length of strip to cut: Multiply the length of the side of the unfinished piece by the number of pieced blocks in the quilt. Add leeway and cut as many strips of each color as there are pieces of that color in one block:
    2.5 × 32 = 80 inches.
        Cut 9 strips of "A" material.
        Cut 16 strips of "B" material, **or preferably, cut 4 strips only** of "B" material for the center nine-patch, and then cut the three pieces on each side which occur together as one, as follows:
        Rows 1 and 5: "B" material
        Cut 2 strips 6.5 by 80 inches.
        Sidestrips: "B" material
        Cut 6 strips 2.5 by 80 inches. Cut into 6.5 inch segments (⅔ strip extra).
Alternate blocks (31): "B" material
    Cut 3 strips 10.5 by 115.5 inches (2 extra blocks).
Borders: Allow 98 inches.
Binding: "A" material.
Backing: Purchase 6 yards of material.

47

B. Sailboats

Plate VII-B.

This quilt is pieced with eight different prints of the same hue and value.

The value of the color of the chains must be the same for the quilt to qualify as an Irish Chain. Variation in prints gives it a special close-up appeal.

Quilt could be made with a variation for every block, or with any combination of variation prints. If each block is different, each square must be cut individually.

This example: Four blocks each of 8 different prints.
Instructions: Section VII-A, with this exception:
2.5 × 4 = 10 inches (add leeway)
Cut 9 strips of each of 8 "A" materials.

Follow cutting layout chart for "B" material. Strips for center 9-patch and for Rows 1 and 5 can be cut into 10 inch (add leeway) segments.

Borders: Pieced scraps of various "A" materials for narrow inner border, or strips left from a backing of "A" material. Borders could be made from "B" material only, with Picot, or Prairie Points of "A" material added for an attractive finishing touch.

The boat pattern was made from a picture in the January, 1935, *National Geographic Magazine*, page 8. The caption under the picture reads, "Trim and graceful as gulls on the wing, they speed over the white-capped waters in one of the close and thrilling races for smaller craft. One holds a slight open-water lead and the others are in hot pursuit." It is a part of an article entitled "England's Sun Trap Isle of Wight" by J.R. Hildebrand, photo by Beken and Son.

The picture was photographed and enlarged. Stencils were cut from waxed stencil paper.

Navy blue and white quilts became popular in the early 20th Century. At one time, about 250 navy blue and white Double Irish Chain quilts were made for the nurses' boarding home of the Children's Mercy Hospital in Kansas City, Missouri.

C. Butterflies, Alternating Background

Plate VII-C.
Quilted by Author.

This Extended Single Chain is achieved by piecing the "A" color chain block with one background color ("B") and alternating it with a plain block of another color ("C").

The chain should be dominant, with the background color of the pieced block dominant over the color of the plain block.
Instructions: VII-A with these exceptions:

Follow cutting layout chart for "B" material for strips for pieced block only. Allow 98 inches for borders. Add allowance for shrinkage and lack of square cut.

Cut each plain block and a 1 inch inside border from a third, or "C" material. Add allowance for purchase.

D. Lemon Star

A different look is achieved by setting the blocks diagonally. An eight point Lemon Star is pieced by hand, to set into each alternate block.

Plate VII-D.

Figures are shown here for Twin size quilt. Directions given for single-print "A" color material (example shows multiprint).

Size: 5 blocks wide and 7 blocks long. No borders.

The size is determined by multiplying the diagonal measure of the finished block by the number of pieced blocks in the width and the length of the quilt. The diagonal of the ten inch square block is 14.14 inches (10 × 10 × 2 = 200. Take the square root).

5 × 14.14 = 70.7 inches (71)

7 × 14.14 = 98.98 inches (99)

Blocks: Quilt top has 35 pieced blocks, 24 star blocks, 20 edge triangles and 4 corner triangles. Each block is 10 inches square finished and 10.5 inches square unfinished.

Piece: 2 inches square finished, and 2.5 inches square unfinished. Three pieces together are 2 by 6 inches finished, and 2.5 by 6.5 inches unfinished.

Instructions: Figure VII-D-1.

Pieced blocks (35).

2.5 × 35 = 87.5

Cut 9 strips "A" material.

Cut 16 strips "B" material, **or preferably, cut 4 strips only** of "B" material for center nine-patch, and then cut the three pieces on each side which occur together, as one:

Rows 1 and 5: ("B" material)

Cut 2 strips 6.5 by 87.5 inches.

Sidestrips: ("B" material)

Cut 6 strips 2.5 by 87.5 inches (extra)

Alternate, or star block (24):

Cut plain blocks of background material 10.5 inches square.

Stars: 192 diamonds of "A" material and 192 squares of "B" material are needed for the stars.

"A" material: 32 inches of 45 inch material, or 66 inches of 19.5 width remnant. Add leeway. (Allow for shrinkage and lack of square cut if purchased separately.)

The pattern (unfinished) used for the stars in this quilt has a 2 inch transverse measure, and a 2.82 ($2^{13}/_{16}$) inch side measure. It is called a 2-inch, 45 degree angle diamond.

The finished side of the star is 2.12 (2⅛) inches. Therefore, the unfinished square to piece into the star must be 2 ⅝ inches. This is represented by "5.6" on the cutting layout chart.

Cut star diamonds with the tip to tip line on the lengthwise grain of the material.

Piece together the eight point star. Set in eight "corners."

Measure the pieced star from tip to tip. Cut a circle in the alternate block ½ inch less than this measure, as follows:

Set compass at a distance ½ the measure, less ¼ inch for the seam allowance. Center the sharp point of the compass in the center of the plain block (determined by press-folding the block in fourths), and draw circle. Cut circle out. Clip a scant ¼ inch, evenly, into edge of circle of plain block, at frequent intervals (as ¼ inch).

Center circle over the pieced star. Set the star tip to tip within the block. Pin. Tuck seam allowance in evenly with finger and needle and blind-stitch. Frame the star exactly at the tip of each point, and in a perfect circle.

Edge Triangles (20): Refer to Section IV-B.

Cut 5 - 15⅝ inch squares of "B" material to be cut into 4 triangles each.

Corner Triangles (4):

Cut 2 - 8¼ inch squares of "B" material to be cut into 2 triangles each.

Setting: Set diagonally. Refer to Section IV-A.

Binding: "A" material.

Backing: Purchase 6¼ yards of material.

EXTENDED SINGLE IRISH CHAIN WITH LEMON STAR

Twin Size 71 x 99 in.

A Color Material

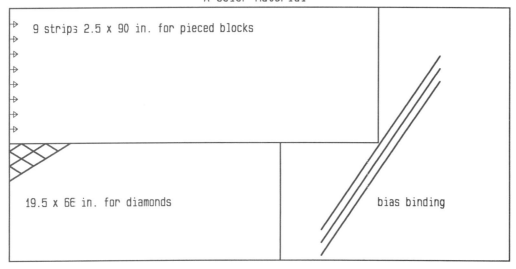

9 strips 2.5 x 90 in. for pieced blocks

19.5 x 66 in. for diamonds

bias binding

Purchase 3 3/8 yards A color material.

B Color Material

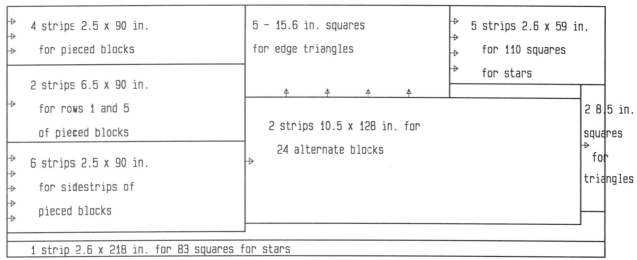

4 strips 2.5 x 90 in.
    for pieced blocks

2 strips 6.5 x 90 in.
    for rows 1 and 5
    of pieced blocks

6 strips 2.5 x 90 in.
    for sidestrips of
    pieced blocks

5 - 15.6 in. squares
for edge triangles

2 strips 10.5 x 128 in. for
24 alternate blocks

5 strips 2.6 x 59 in.
    for 110 squares
    for stars

2 8.5 in.
squares
    for
triangles

1 strip 2.6 x 218 in. for 83 squares for stars

Purchase 6 7/8 yards B color material.

Figure VII-D-1

Plate VII-E.

E. Old Tulip Applique Medallion

A Medallion should be coordinated with the size of the blocks, to keep the continuity of the Irish Chain pattern. The blocks are set on the diagonal to accommodate the Medallion.

The pattern and relationship of blocks is shown in Section IV-A, Figure IV-A-2.

Figures shown here are for a Double size quilt.

Size: 5 pieced blocks wide and 7 pieced blocks long, with 5 inch appliqued borders. The size is determined by multiplying the diagonal of the finished block (14.14) by the number of pieced blocks in the width and the length of the quilt and adding the width of the borders.

70.7 plus 5 inch borders = 80.7 (81) inches

98.98 plus 5 inch borders = 108.98 (109) inches

Blocks: Quilt has 30 pieced blocks, 20 alternate blocks, 20 edge triangles, and 4 corner triangles. Blocks are 10 inches square finished, and 10.5 inches square finished.

Piece: 2 inches finished, 2.5 inches unfinished. Three pieces together are 2 by 6 inches finished and 2.5 by 6.5 inches unfinished.

Medallion: 30.5 inches square.

The medallion replaces 5 pieced and 4 alternate blocks. The size of the medallion is determined by multiplying the length of the side of the finished block by three, and adding seam allowances.

Applique: Pattern of choice and one or more additional colors. (Classic pattern for Old Tulip can be found in *Quilts*, Book No. 190, published by the Spool Cotton Co. in 1942.)

Instructions: Figure VII-E-1.

Add leeway to length of strip listed in text.

Pieced blocks (30):

$2.5 \times 30 = 75$ inches

Cut 9 strips of "A" material.

Cut 4 strips of "B" material (center).

Cut 2 strips of "B" material 6.5 inches wide for Rows 1 and 5.

Sidestrips: "B" material

Cut 6 strips 2.5 by 65 inches. Cut into 6.5 inch segments.

Alternate Blocks (20): "B" material

Cut 3 strips 10.5 by 73.5 inches.

Medallion: "B" material

Cut one 30.5 inch square.

Edge Triangles (20): "B" material. Refer to Section IV-B.

Cut 5 - 15⅝ inch squares of "B" material to be cut into 4 triangles each.

Corner Triangles (4):

Cut 2 - 8¼ inch squares of "B" material to be cut into 2 triangles each.

Borders: Cut 2 strips 5.5 by 112 inches and 2 strips 5.5 by 84 inches for borders.

Binding: "A" material.

Backing: Purchase 6¾ yards of material.

MEDALLION

EXTENDED SINGLE IRISH CHAIN

with OLD TULIP APPLIQUE

Double Size 81 x 109 in.

A Color Material

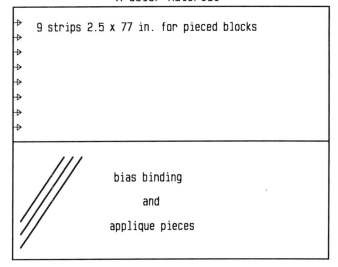

9 strips 2.5 x 77 in. for pieced blocks

bias binding
and
applique pieces

Purchase 2 1/2 yards A color material

B Color Material

(Cut medallion and all strips first)

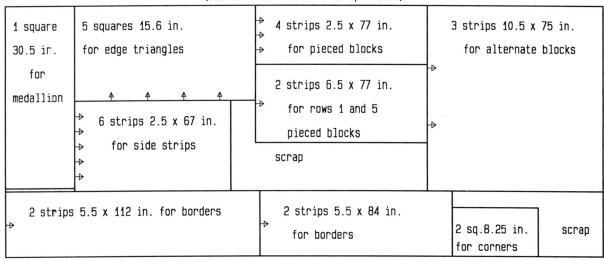

1 square 30.5 in. for medallion

5 squares 15.6 in. for edge triangles

4 strips 2.5 x 77 in. for pieced blocks

3 strips 10.5 x 75 in. for alternate blocks

6 strips 2.5 x 67 in. for side strips

2 strips 6.5 x 77 in. for rows 1 and 5 pieced blocks

scrap

2 strips 5.5 x 112 in. for borders

2 strips 5.5 x 84 in. for borders

2 sq. 8.25 in. for corners

scrap

Purchase 7 7/8 yards B color material.

Purchase 1/4 yard C color material for applique.

Figure VII-E-1

Plate VII-F.

F. Covered Bridge Applique Medallion

The Medallion Quilt can readily be used to feature a personal or commemorative motif. The Covered Bridge in this quilt is a commercial pattern from the Quail Roost Studio, Stuart, Florida. It is surrounded by four classic tree blocks, and quilted with an ivy leaf, reminiscent of the state of Maine.

The diagonal set appears well with medium borders with decorative motifs, or with no borders whatsoever. Narrow borders do not appear well.

Figures are shown here for a Double Queen size quilt.

Size: 7 pieced blocks × 12.37 = 86.6 inches

9 pieced blocks × 12.37 = 111.33 inches

Blocks: Quilt top has 58 pieced blocks, 44 alternate blocks, 28 edge triangles and 4 corner triangles. Blocks are 8.75 inches square finished and 9.25 inches square unfinished. The diagonal measure of 8.75 inch square is 12.37.

Piece: 1.75 inches finished, 2.25 inches unfinished.

Medallion: 26.25 inches square finished, 26.75 inches square unfinished

Applique: Pattern of choice and one or more additional colors.

Instructions: Figure VII-F-I.

Add leeway to length of strip listed in text.

Pieced blocks (58):

2.25 × 58 = 130.5 inches

Cut 9 strips "A" material.

Cut 4 strips "B" material (center).

Rows 1 and 5: "B" material

Cut two strips 5.75 by 130.5 inches.

Sidestrips: "B" material

Cut 6 strips 2.25 by 115 inches. Cut into 5.75 inch segments (partial strip extra).

Alternate Blocks: (44) "B" material

Cut 1 strip 9.25 by 148 inches for 16 alternate blocks.

Cut 1 strip 9.25 by 157.25 inches for 17 alternate blocks.

Cut 4 strips 9.25 by 27.75 inches for 11 alternate blocks (1 extra).

Medallion: "B" material

Cut 1 - 26.75 inch square to receive applique.

The Picture Center including individual borders measure 14.14 inches, finished. This figure divided by 2 (7.07 inches) equals the hypotenuse edge of the triangle.

The equal edge of the triangle and the side of the square are 5 inches. (7.07 × 7.07 ÷ 2 = 24.99. Take the square root, which equals 5).

The diagonal of the inside square (20 inches) subtracted from the side of the Medallion square (26.25) gives the combined width of the borders (6.25 inches). Each border will be 3⅛ inch wide. Add seam allowance.

Cut 4 border strips 3⅝ inches wide and 27.75 inches (includes leeway) long. Attach. Miter corners.

Edge Triangles (28): "B" material.

Cut 7 - 13¾ inch squares for 28 edge triangles.

Corner Triangles (4):

Cut 2 - 7.25 inch squares to be cut into two triangles each.

Borders: None.

Binding: "A" material.

Backing: (1) Purchase 10¼ yards (3 lengths), or (2) Coordinate with material for top. Purchase 2 lengths according to formula (7 yards) and use the lower 8 inches on the cutting layout chart for "B" material for 2 strips to supplement the backing.

MEDALLION

EXTENDED SINGLE IRISH CHAIN WITH COVERED BRIDGE APPLIQUE

Double Queen Size 87 x 112 in.

A Color Material

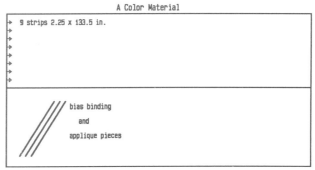

Purchase 4 yards A color material.

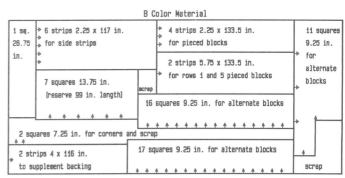

Purchase 9 yards B color material.

Figure VII-F-1

Plate VIII-A.

VIII.
Double Irish Chain I

A. Brown and Gold

The Double Irish Chain is commonly constructed with a 25-patch block and an alternate block with 4 set-in corners. Figure VIII-A-1.

```
A B C B A  B        B

B A B A B

C B A B C     C

B A B A B

A B C B A  B        B
```

Figure VIII-A-1

Each pieced block contains:
    9 squares "A" material
    12 squares "B" material
    4 squares "C" material
Each alternate block is "C" material with a square of "B" material in each corner.
    Figures are shown here for Twin Double size quilt:
    Size: 7 blocks wide and 9 blocks long
        70 plus 2.5 inch borders = 75 inches
        90 plus 2.5 inch borders = 95 inches
Blocks: Quilt top has 63 blocks with 32 pieced and 31 alternate blocks. Each block is 10 inches square finished and 10.5 inches square unfinished.
    Piece: 2 inches square finished, and 2.5 inches square unfinished.

Plate VIII-A.

Instructions: See Figures VIII-A-2.1, 2.2.

DOUBLE IRISH CHAIN I

Twin Double Size 75 x 95 in.

A Color Material

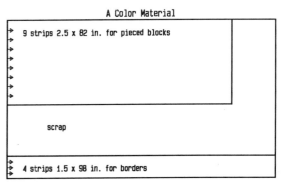

9 strips 2.5 x 82 in. for pieced blocks

scrap

4 strips 1.5 x 98 in. for borders

Purchase 3 1/8 yards A material.

B Color Material

12 strips 2.5 x 82 in. for pieced blocks

8 strips 2.5 x 41 in. for corners of alternate blocks

scrap

4 strips 2.5 x 98 in. for borders

Purchase 3 7/8 yards B color material.
Purchase 1/2 yard extra for binding.

Figure VIII-A-2.1

DOUBLE IRISH CHAIN I

Twin Double Size 75 x 95 in.

C Color Material

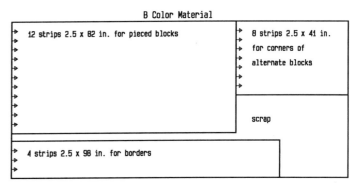

4 strips 2.5 x 82 in. for pieced blocks

4 strips 6.5 x 41 in. for rows 1 and 5

4 strips 6.5 x 53 in. for centers for alternate blocks

scrap

6 strips 2.5 x 53 in. for side strips

scrap

2 strips 2.5 x 53 in.

Purchase 3 7/8 yards C color material.
Figure VIII-A-2.2

Corners will be set in alternate block by Strip Method, Section III-D.

Add leeway to length of strip listed in text.

Pieced Blocks (32):

Multiply the length of the side of one unfinished square by the number of pieced blocks in the quilt for the length of strip to cut for all blocks. Cut as many strips of each color as there are pieces of that color in one block:

2.5 × 32 = 80 inches

    Cut 9 strips of "A" material.
    Cut 12 strips of "B" material.
    Cut 4 strips of "C" material.

Alternate Blocks (31):

  Centers: "C" material

    Cut 4 strips 6.5 by 52 inches.

  Sidestrips: "C" material

    Cut 8 strips 2.5 by 52 inches.

  Row 1 and 5:

    Corner squares: "B" material

    2.5 × 31 = 77.5 inches. Cut 4 strips, **or preferably,** cut twice as many strips one-half as long (38.75). Increase to next multiple of 2.5 inches.

    Cut 8 strips 40 inches in length.

  Center of Rows 1 and 5: "C" material

    Cut 4 strips 6.5 by 40 inches to correspond with the strip length used for the corners above.

Borders: Allow 98 inches.

Binding: "A" or "B" material.

Backing: Purchase 6 yards of material.

Figures for Double Irish Chain I Queen size quilt:

  Size: 9 blocks wide and 11 blocks long
         90 plus 2.5 inch borders = 95 inches
         110 plus 2.5 inch borders = 115 inches

Blocks: Quilt top has 99 blocks, 50 pieced and 49 alternate. Each block is 10 square finished and 10.5 inches square unfinished.

Piece: 2 inches square finished, and 2.5 inches square unfinished.

  Instructions:

    Add leeway to length of strip listed in text.

    The preferred method for construction of the alternate block is the use of the whole (10.5 inch) block, with pieced in corners. "B" material required for this method is slightly less than for Strip Method. See Section III-C.

    The Wine and Gold quilt (Twin Double size), Plate VIII-A-1, is constructed with pieced-in corners.

    Pieced Blocks (50):

    2.5 × 50 = 125 inches

      Cut 9 strips of "A" material.
      Cut 12 strips of "B" material.
      Cut 4 strips of "C" material.

Alternate Blocks:

    Cut 49 - 10.5 inch squares of "C" material.
    Corner squares: "B" material
    2.5 × 49 = 122.5 inches. Cut 4 strips, **or preferably,**
    Cut 8 strips 62.5 inches long.

Borders: Allow 118 inches.

Binding: "B" material. Purchase ½ yard extra.

Backing: Purchase 10.5 yards of material.

Top: Purchase 4 yards "A" material, 5.75 yards "B" material (6.25 yards will include binding), and 5.5 yards "C" material.

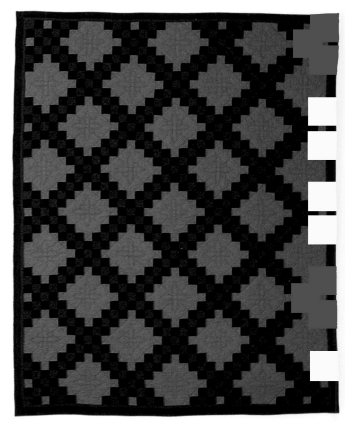

Plate VIII-A-1.

B. Tahoe - A Rainbow Quilt in Sea Greens

I have named this particular quilt TAHOE. My inspiration for it was a picture of our 10-year-old daughter riding the waves of Lake Tahoe on an air mattress.

In the photograph, there is the gray of sand and the light green of dune grass, into the green blue of shallow water. As the water deepens, the shades of blue intensify, and as the distance increases the water picks up some purple. On the far shore are the dark, dark green pine trees.

In the quilt, I began with pine trees in the foreground also (reading from the lower right corner) followed by green-gray plain and prints for shore foliage and sand. The turquoise and avocado stripe blend for a water-color. Then imagination reigns, for swirly deep turquoise and even purple water foliage (which really is not found in Lake Tahoe).

Plate VIII-B.

The plains and prints deepen in value for the expanse of deep water. They would really become darker and blend with the far shore, but in my mind's eye I envision sea monsters, the exotic prints in the set of three blocks. (Our daughter always excitedly pointed out the imaginary pirhana fish in the lake (the sun sparkled crests of the waves).

Beyond is deep gray foliage for sand and shrubs, then dark, dark green for pine trees again.

The plain colors are mostly a collection of sea greens, purchased as such. Part of the prints were salvaged from a collection of used clothing, and part are new. Some of the prints are repeated three times to make the wide, deep part of the lake. However, a general plan can be set up for the six sets of blocks, and they can be pieced by the strata method. Blocks are numbered as follows:

A - 1 block - piece separately
B - 3 blocks
C - 5 blocks
D - 7 blocks
E - 7 blocks
F - 5 blocks
G - 3 blocks
H - 1 block - piece separately

The color pattern is shown in Figure VIII-B-1, labeled Rainbow Block Color Chart. Each rainbow plain color is flanked by coordinate color prints. Each color run is given a separate label (A, B, C, etc.). Color repeats would be at the choice of the maker.

Figures are shown here for a Double size quilt:
Size: 7 blocks wide and 9 blocks long
         78.75 plus inch borders = 83.75 inches
         101.25 plus 2.5 inch borders = 106.25 inches
Blocks: Quilt top has 63 blocks, 32 pieced and 31 alternate, 11.25 inches finished, and 11.75 inches unfinished.
Piece: 2.25 inches square finished, and 2.75 inches unfinished.
Instructions: See Figures VIII-B-2.1, 2.2, 2.3.
    Charts show exact amount of material needed for the various colors. Add for shrinkage and lack of square cut at the purchase counter.
    Corners will be pieced into alternate blocks. Refer to Section III-C.
    Pieced Blocks:
    Since A and H blocks will be pieced individually, detailed instructions will be given for blocks B through G only. Leeway is indicated as "+ 1".
B Block - three blocks
    $2.75 \times 3 = 8.25 + .75 = 9$ inches each strip
        "c" color - 2 strips   "2" print - 2 strips
        "d" color - 5 strips   "3" print - 8 strips
        "e" color - 2 strips   "4" print - 2 strips
C Block - five blocks
    $2.75 \times 5 = 13.75 + 1 = 14.75$ inches each strip

"e" color - 2 strips   "4" print - 2 strips
"f" color - 5 strips   "5" print - 8 strips
"g" color - 2 strips   "6" print - 2 strips
D Block - seven blocks
    $2.75 \times 7 = 19.25 + 1 = 20.25$ inches each strip
        "g" color - 2 strips   "6" print - 2 strips
        "h" color - 5 strips   "7" print - 8 strips
        "i" color - 2 strips   "8" print - 2 strips
E Block - seven blocks
    $2.75 \times 7 = 19.25 + 1 = 20.25$ inches each strip
        "i" color - 2 strips   "8" print - 2 strips
        "j" color - 5 strips   "9" print - 8 strips
        "k" color - 2 strips   "10" print - 2 strips
F Block - 5 blocks
    $2.75 \times 5 = 13.75 + 1 = 14.75$ inches each strip
        "k" color - 2 strips   "10" print - 2 strips
        "l" color - 5 strips   "11" print - 8 strips
        "m" color - 2 strips   "12" print - 2 strips
G Block - 3 blocks
    $2.75 \times 3 = 8.25 + .75 = 9$ inches each strip
        "m" color - 2 strips   "12" print - 2 strips
        "n" color - 5 strips   "13" print - 8 strips
        "p" color - 2 strips   "14" print - 2 strips

A Block will have 2, 5 and 2 pieces of colors "a," "b" and "c," and 2, 8 and 2 pieces, respectively, of its three prints, which are "16," "1" and "2."

H Block will have 2, 5 and 2 pieces of colors "p," "q" and "r," and 2, 8 and 2 pieces, respectively, of its three prints, which are "14," "15" and "16".

The **background** of the pieced block (the same color as the alternate blocks) is represented by color "o." There are 4 pieces in each pieced block: $2.75 \times 32 = 88$ inches. Cut 4 strips of "o" material (no chart).

Alternate blocks: Cut 31 — 11.75 inch squares of the background or "o" color material (no chart).

Please refer to Figure VIII-B-2 for directions for cutting strips and pieces for pieced and alternate blocks.

Alternate blocks also require pieces as follows:

Print 1 -   2 pieces   Print 9 - 13 pieces
Print 2 -   4 pieces   Print 10 - 12 pieces
Print 3 -   6 pieces   Print 11 - 10 pieces
Print 4 -   8 pieces   Print 12 - 8 pieces
Print 5 - 10 pieces   Print 13 - 6 pieces
Print 6 - 12 pieces   Print 14 - 4 pieces
Print 7 - 13 pieces   Print 15 - 2 pieces
Print 8 - 14 pieces

Borders: Allow 109.25 inches.
    Cut 1 inch borders of "o" material, 1.25 inch borders of a deeper color, and 1.75 inch borders of another deep plain or print.
Binding: By choice.
Backing: Purchase 6¾ yards.

RAINBOW BLOCK COLOR CHART

```
        A                      B                      C                      D

r 16 o 1 b │1          2│c 2 o 3 d │3        4│e 4 o 5 f│5        6│g 6 o 7 h
16 a 1 b 1 │           │2 c 3 d 3 │         │4 e 5 f 5│         │6 g 7 h 7
o 1 b 1 o  │     o     │o 3 d 3 o │   o     │o 5 f 5 o│   o     │o 7 h 7 o
1 b 1 c 2  │           │3 d 3 e 4 │         │5 f 5 g 6│         │7 h 7 i 8
b 1 o 2 c  │2          3│d 3 o 4 e│4       5│f 5 o 6 g│6       7│h 7 o 8 i
──────────────────────────────────────────────────────────────────────────
1          2│c 2 o 3 d │3        4│e 4 o 5 f│5        6│g 6 o 7 h│7         8
            │2 c 3 d 3 │         │4 e 5 f 5│         │6 g 7 h 7│
            │o 3 d 3 o │         │o 5 f 5 o│         │o 7 h 7 o│
            │3 d 3 e 4 │         │5 f 5 g 6│         │7 h 7 i 8│
2          3│d 3 o 4 e│4       5│f 5 o 6 g│6       7│h 7 o 8 i│8         9
──────────────────────────────────────────────────────────────────────────
c 2 o 3 d │3        4│e 4 o 5 f│5        6│g 6 o 7 h│7        8│i 8 o 9 j│ E
2 c 3 d 3 │         │4 e 5 f 5│         │6 g 7 h 7│         │8 i 9 j 9
o 3 d 3 o │         │o 5 f 5 o│         │o 7 h 7 o│         │o 9 j 9 o
3 d 3 e 4 │         │5 f 5 g 6│         │7 h 7 i 8│         │9 j 9 k 10
d 3 o 4 e│4       5│f 5 o 6 g│6       7│h 7 o 8 i│8       9│j 9 o 10 k
──────────────────────────────────────────────────────────────────────────
3        4│e 4 o 5 f│5        6│g 6 o 7 h│7        8│i 8 o 9 j│9        10
          │4 e 5 f 5│         │6 g 7 h 7│         │8 i 9 j 9│
          │o 5 f 5 o│         │o 7 h 7 o│         │o 9 j 9 o│
          │5 f 5 g 6│         │7 h 7 i 8│         │9 j 9 k 10│
4       5│f 5 o 6 g│6       7│h 7 o 8 i│8       9│j 9 o 10 k│10       11
──────────────────────────────────────────────────────────────────────────
e 4 o 5 f│5        6│g 6 o 7 h│7        8│i 8 o 9 j│g        10│k 10 o 11 l│ F
4 e 5 f 5│         │6 g 7 h 7│         │8 i 9 j 9│          │10 k 11 l 11
o 5 f 5 o│         │o 7 h 7 o│         │o 9 j 9 o│          │o 11 l 11 o
5 f 5 g 6│         │7 h 7 i 8│         │9 j 9 k 10│          │11 l 11 m 12
f 5 o 6 g│6       7│h 7 o 8 i│8       9│j 9 o 10 k│10       11│l 11 o 12 m
──────────────────────────────────────────────────────────────────────────
5        6│g 6 o 7 h│7        8│i 8 o 9 j│9        10│k 10 o 11 l│15       12
          │6 g 7 h 7│         │8 i 9 j 9│          │10 k 11 l 11│
          │o 7 h 7 o│         │o 9 j 9 o│          │o 11 l 11 o│
          │7 h 7 i 8│         │9 j 9 k 10│          │11 l 11 m 12│
6       7│h 7 o 8 i│8       9│j 9 o 10 k│10       11│l 11 o 12 m│12       13
──────────────────────────────────────────────────────────────────────────
g 6 o 7 h│7        8│i 8 o 9 j│9        10│k 10 o 11 l│11       12│m 12 o 13 n│ G
6 g 7 h 7│         │8 i 9 j 9│          │10 k 11 l 11│         │12 m 13 n 13
o 7 h 7 o│         │o 9 j 9 o│          │o 11 l 11 o│         │o 13 n 13 o
7 h 7 i 8│         │9 j 9 k 10│          │11 l 11 m 12│         │13 n 13 p 14
h 7 o 8 i│8       9│j 9 o 10 k│10       11│l 11 o 12 m│12      13│n 13 o 14 p
──────────────────────────────────────────────────────────────────────────
7        8│i 8 o 9 j│9        10│k 10 o 11 l│11       12│m 12 o 13 n│13       14
          │8 i 9 j 9│          │10 k 11 l 11│         │12 m 13 n 13│
          │o 9 j 9 o│          │o 11 l 11 o│         │o 13 n 13 o│
          │9 j 9 k 10│          │11 l 11 m 12│         │13 n 13 p 14│
8       9│j 9 o 10 k│10       11│l 11 o 12 m│12      13│n 13 o 14 p│14       15
──────────────────────────────────────────────────────────────────────────
i 8 o 9 j│9        10│k 10 o 11 l│11       12│m 12 o 13 n│13       14│p 14 o 15 q│ H
8 i 9 j 9│          │10 k 11 l 11│         │12 m 13 n 13│         │14 p 15 q 15
o 9 j 9 o│          │o 11 l 11 o│         │o 13 n 13 o│         │o 15 q 15 o
9 j 9 k 10│          │11 l 11 m 12│         │13 n 13 p 14│         │15 q 15 r 16
j 9 o 10 k│10       11│l 11 o 12 m│12      13│n 13 o 14 p│14      15│q 15 o 16 r
```

Figure VIII-B-1

RAINBOW QUILT

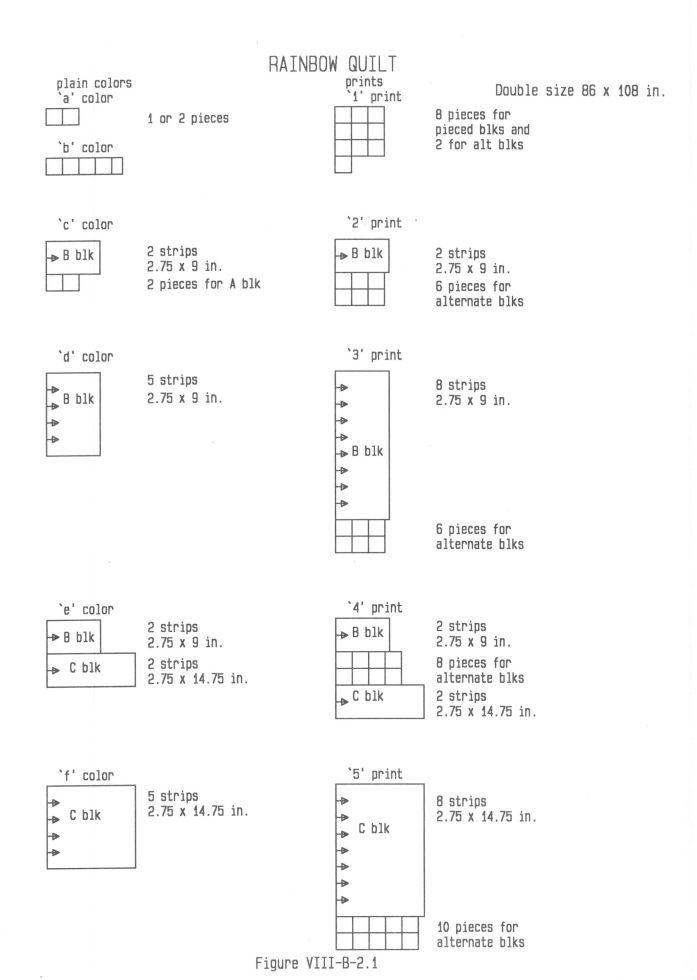

plain colors
`a' color
1 or 2 pieces

`b' color

prints
`1' print
8 pieces for
pieced blks and
2 for alt blks

Double size 86 x 108 in.

`c' color
B blk
2 strips
2.75 x 9 in.
2 pieces for A blk

`2' print
B blk
2 strips
2.75 x 9 in.
6 pieces for
alternate blks

`d' color
B blk
5 strips
2.75 x 9 in.

`3' print
B blk
8 strips
2.75 x 9 in.

6 pieces for
alternate blks

`e' color
B blk
C blk
2 strips
2.75 x 9 in.
2 strips
2.75 x 14.75 in.

`4' print
B blk
C blk
2 strips
2.75 x 9 in.
8 pieces for
alternate blks
2 strips
2.75 x 14.75 in.

`f' color
C blk
5 strips
2.75 x 14.75 in.

`5' print
C blk
8 strips
2.75 x 14.75 in.

10 pieces for
alternate blks

Figure VIII-B-2.1

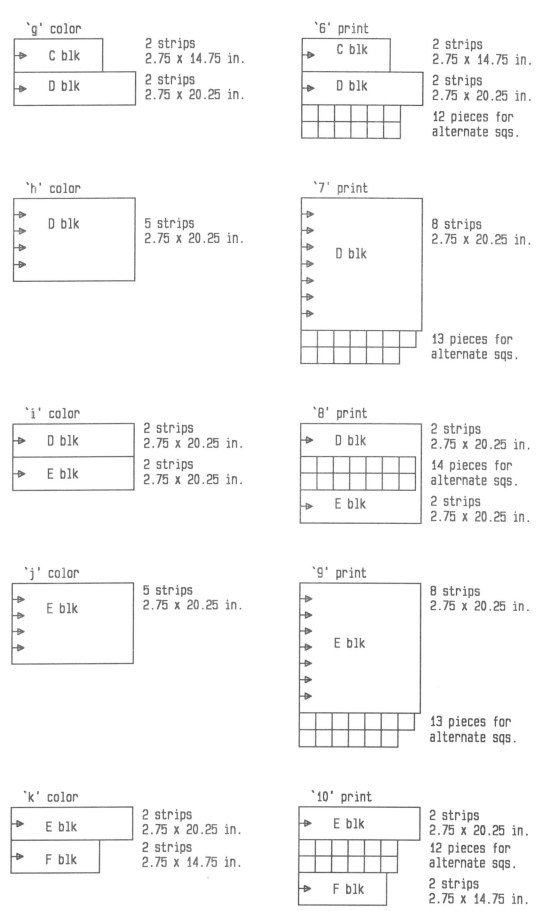

'g' color

C blk — 2 strips 2.75 x 14.75 in.

D blk — 2 strips 2.75 x 20.25 in.

'6' print

C blk — 2 strips 2.75 x 14.75 in.

D blk — 2 strips 2.75 x 20.25 in.

12 pieces for alternate sqs.

'h' color

D blk — 5 strips 2.75 x 20.25 in.

'7' print

D blk — 8 strips 2.75 x 20.25 in.

13 pieces for alternate sqs.

'i' color

D blk — 2 strips 2.75 x 20.25 in.

E blk — 2 strips 2.75 x 20.25 in.

'8' print

D blk — 2 strips 2.75 x 20.25 in.

14 pieces for alternate sqs.

E blk — 2 strips 2.75 x 20.25 in.

'j' color

E blk — 5 strips 2.75 x 20.25 in.

'9' print

E blk — 8 strips 2.75 x 20.25 in.

13 pieces for alternate sqs.

'k' color

E blk — 2 strips 2.75 x 20.25 in.

F blk — 2 strips 2.75 x 14.75 in.

'10' print

E blk — 2 strips 2.75 x 20.25 in.

12 pieces for alternate sqs.

F blk — 2 strips 2.75 x 14.75 in.

Figure VIII-B-2.2

61

62

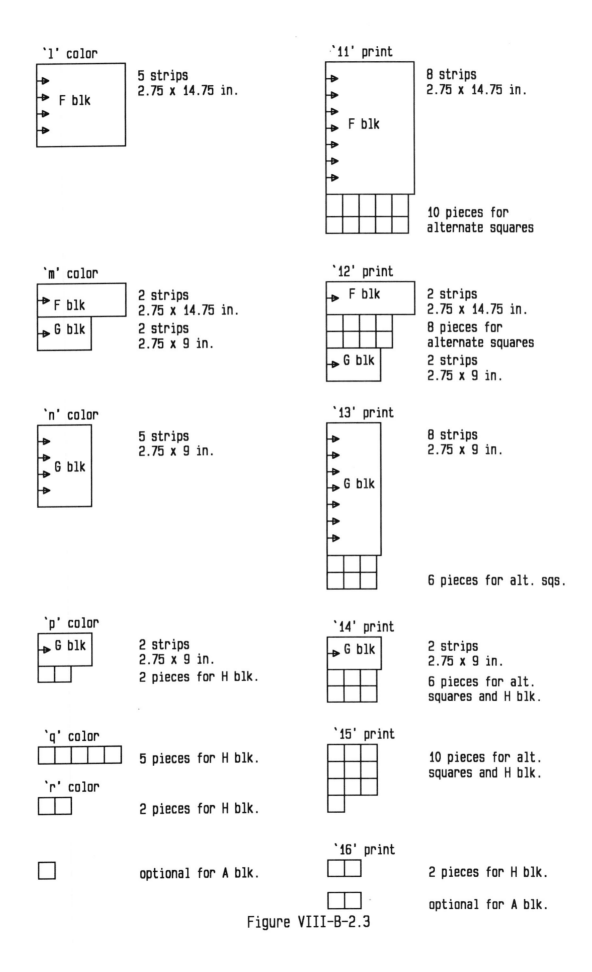

'l' color — F blk — 5 strips 2.75 x 14.75 in.

'11' print — F blk — 8 strips 2.75 x 14.75 in.

10 pieces for alternate squares

'm' color — F blk / G blk — 2 strips 2.75 x 14.75 in. / 2 strips 2.75 x 9 in.

'12' print — F blk / G blk — 2 strips 2.75 x 14.75 in. / 8 pieces for alternate squares / 2 strips 2.75 x 9 in.

'n' color — G blk — 5 strips 2.75 x 9 in.

'13' print — G blk — 8 strips 2.75 x 9 in.

6 pieces for alt. sqs.

'p' color — G blk — 2 strips 2.75 x 9 in. / 2 pieces for H blk.

'14' print — G blk — 2 strips 2.75 x 9 in. / 6 pieces for alt. squares and H blk.

'q' color — 5 pieces for H blk.

'r' color — 2 pieces for H blk.

'15' print — 10 pieces for alt. squares and H blk.

optional for A blk.

'16' print — 2 pieces for H blk.

optional for A blk.

Figure VIII-B-2.3

IX.
Extended Double Irish Chain II

A. Orchid, Turquoise and Rose

Plate IX-A.

The Double Irish Chain may also be seen in a long graceful form which may be accomplished with a 49-patch block. Figure IX-A-1.*

A	B	C		B	A	B			B
B	A	B	C	B	A	B			
	B	A	B	A	B				
C	C	B	A	B	C	C		C	
	B	A	B	A	B				
B	A	B	C	B	A	B			
A	B	C		B	A	B			B

Figure IX-A-1

Each pieced block contains:
13 squares "A" material
20 squares "B" material
16 squares "C" material
    Three squares of one color occurring together will be cut as one piece.

*The Farmer's Wife Magazine, Quilts, New Patterns and Designs by Orinne Johnson, Webb Publishing Co., St. Paul, MN 1937, p. 1. (rep. Barbara Bannister, Alanson MI, 1982)

Each alternate block of "C" material has a square of "B" material in each corner.

Figures are shown here for a Queen size quilt.
    Size: 7 blocks wide and 9 blocks long
        85.75 plus 2.5 inch borders = 90.75 inches
        110.25 plus 2.5 inch borders = 115.25 inches
    Blocks: Quilt top has 63 blocks with 32 pieced and 31 alternate blocks. Each block is 12.25 inches square, finished and 12.75 inches square unfinished.
    Piece: 1.75 inches square finished and 2.25 inches unfinished. Three pieces together are 1.75 × 5.25 finished and 2.25 × 5.75 inches unfinished.
Instructions: Figure IX-A-2.
    Add leeway to length of strip listed in text.
    Corners will be pieced into alternate blocks. Section III-C.
    Pieced Blocks (32): Construct center section (Rows 3, 4 and 5). Add sidestrips. Add Rows 2 and 6. Add Rows 1 and 7.
Pressing Seams: See Section III-B-3-c.
Calculate the length of strip to cut: Multiply the length of the side of the unfinished piece by the number of pieced blocks in the quilt to determine the length of strip to cut for all blocks. Cut as many strips of each color as there are pieces of that color in one block:
    2.25 × 32 = 72 inches
    Cut 13 strips "A" material.
    Cut 20 strips "B" material.
    Cut 16 strips "C" material, **or, preferably,**
        Cut 4 strips only of "C" material for Rows 2, 6 and 4, and then cut the three squares on each side which occur together as one, as follows:
    Rows 1 and 7: ("C" material)
        Cut 2 strips 5.75 by 72 inches.
    Sidestrips: ("C" material)
        Cut 6 strips 2.25 by 72 inches.
        Cut into 5.75 inch segments (partial strip extra).
Alternate Blocks (31):
    Blocks: "C" material
        Cut 3 strips 12.75 by 140.25 inches (2 extra).
    Corner Squares: ("B" material)
        Cut 4 strips 2.25 by 69.75 inches.
        Cut into 2.25 inch pieces for insertion into the alternate block.
Borders: Allow 118.5 inches.
Binding: "A" material.
Backing: Purchase 10.5 yards of material (3 lengths).

EXTENDED DOUBLE
IRISH CHAIN II

Queen Size 91 x 115 in.

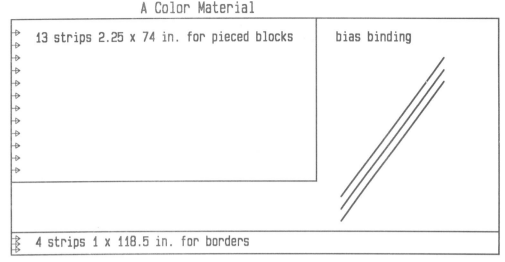

A Color Material

13 strips 2.25 x 74 in. for pieced blocks

bias binding

4 strips 1 x 118.5 in. for borders

Purchase 3 3/4 yards of A color material.

B Color Material

10 strips 2.25 x 74 in. for pieced blocks

10 strips 2.25 x 74 in. for pieced blocks

4 strips 2.25 x 72 in. for
plain block corners

scrap

4 strips 2.25 x 118.5 in. for borders

Purchase 4 1/2 yards of B color material.

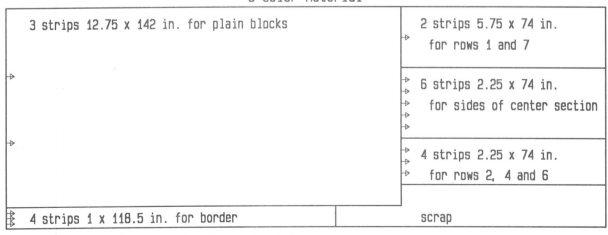

C Color Material

3 strips 12.75 x 142 in. for plain blocks

2 strips 5.75 x 74 in.
for rows 1 and 7

6 strips 2.25 x 74 in.
for sides of center section

4 strips 2.25 x 74 in.
for rows 2, 4 and 6

4 strips 1 x 118.5 in. for border

scrap

Purchase 6 1/2 yards C color material.

Figure IX-A-2

X.
Introduction to Triple Irish Chains

The term "triple" of the Irish Chain refers to the three single chains, set side by side. An identical alternate line of color separates the three chains.

A Triple Irish Chain has complete continuity of color if there are only two colors in the chains, and a third color for the background. (Example: Triple Irish I - Pink and Purple Quilt with Black Paisley background. Section XI-A.)

Plate XI-A.

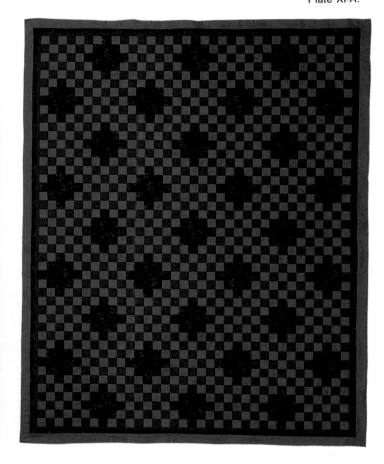

A completely different effect is achieved if the background is the same color as one of the colors of the chains (two colors in complete quilt). (Example: Triple Irish III - Turquoise and White Quilt. Section XIII-A.)

A "'Round the World" effect is made if there are three colors in the chain with a fourth color for the background. The third color of the chain cannot continue through the block. Rather, it frames the plain space. (Example: Triple Irish II - Lavender, Wine and Fig Quilt. Section XII-A.)

Any of these three color combinations can be made into:

1. A Simple Triple Irish (I) (two squares between turning squares). (Example: Pink, Purple and Black Quilt. Section XI.) Figure X-1.

2. An Extended Triple Irish (II) (four squares bet-

ween turning squares). (Example: Lavender, Wine and Fig Quilt. Section XII.) Figure X-2.

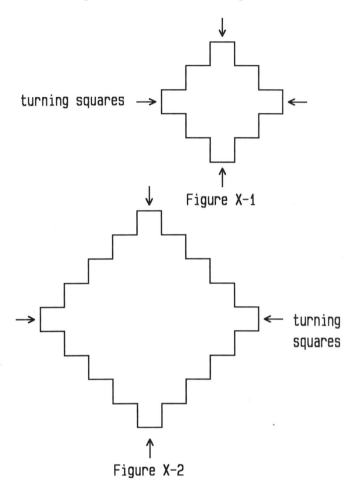

turning squares →

Figure X-1

→

turning squares

Figure X-2

3. An Extended Triple Irish (III) (six squares between turning squares). (Example: Turquoise and White Quilt. Section XIII.)

4. An Extended Triple Irish IV (eight squares between turning squares). (Example: Blue, Brown and White Quilt. Section XIV.)

The Roman Numeral labeling of the Triple Irish Chain Patterns refers to the degree of extension of the chain. The pieced block in each type requires:

Triple Irish I - 25 piece block (2-point Triple)
Triple Irish II - 49 piece block (4-point Triple)
Triple Irish III - 81 piece block (6-point Triple)
Triple Irish IV - 121 piece block (8-point Triple)
Triple Irish V - 169 piece block (10-point Triple). Not shown in this study. A picture of one block is shown in *Woman's Day*, July 1982, pp. 66, 69).

The less "points" in the chain, the more necessary it is to "piece in" the corners. Triple Irish Chains III and IV are fine with strip-pieced alternate blocks or sashing. (Refer Sections III-C, III-D and III-E.)

XI.
Triple Irish Chain I

A. Purple, Rose and Black Paisley

This is the simplest form of the Triple Irish Chain. Figure XI-A-1.

Figure XI-A-1

(See Note for directions for three colors in the chain.)

Each pieced block contains:
13 squares "A" material
12 squares "B" material
Each alternate block is "C" material and contains:
8 squares "A" material
4 squares "B" material
Figures are shown here for a Double size quilt:
Size: 7 blocks wide and 9 blocks long
70 plus 3.5 borders = 77 inches
90 plus 3.5 borders = 97 inches
Blocks: Quilt top has 63 blocks with 32 pieced and 31 alternate blocks, each 10 inches squares finished, and 10.5 inches square unfinished.
Piece: 2 inches square finished and 2.5 inches square unfinished.
Instructions: See Figures XI-A-2.1, 2.2.
Add leeway to length of strip listed in text.
Corners will be pieced into alternate blocks.
Section III-C.

Pieced Blocks (32):
Calculate the length of strip to cut: Multiply the length of the side of the unfinished piece by the number of pieced blocks in the quilt to determine the length of strip needed for all blocks. Cut as many strips of each color as there are pieces of that color in one block:
2.5 × 32 = 80 inches (add leeway)
Cut 13 strips "A" material.
Cut 12 strips "B" material.
Alternate Blocks (31):
Blocks: "C" material
Cut 3 strips 10.5 by 115.5 inches (2 blocks extra).
Corner Squares (8): "A" material
Calculate total length of strip needed (620 in-

TRIPLE IRISH CHAIN I

Double Size 77 x 97 in.

A Color Material

Purchase 4 1/8 yards A color material.

B Color Material

Purchase 3 1/4 yards B color material.
Figure XI-A-2.1

TRIPLE IRISH CHAIN I

Double Size 77 x 97 in.

C Color Material

Purchase 3 5/8 yards C color material.
Figure XI-A-2.2

Plate XI-A.

ches). Divide by number of strips which may be cut in material available (13). Increase to next multiple of one piece.

    Cut 13 strips 2.5 by 50 inches.

Corner squares (4): "B" material:

  Total strip needed: 310 inches.

  Use 1 strip that is available in the 82 inch length and cut 13 strips 2.5 by 20 inches.

    Cut into 2.5 inch squares for insertion into alternate blocks

Borders: Allow 100 inches for borders.

Binding: Purchase separately.

Backing: Purchase 6 yards of material.

Note: Three colors in chain: Pieced block requires 9 squares "A," 12 squares "B," and 4 squares "C" material. Alternate Block requires 4 squares "B" material and 8 squares "C" material. Figure XI-A-3.

A	B	C	B	A	B	C		C	B
B	A	B	A	B	C				C
C	B	A	B	C					
B	A	B	A	B	C				C
A	B	C	B	A	B	C		C	B

Figure XI-A-3

XII.
Extended Triple Irish Chain II

The example quilt has a spot-cut flower motif in the "A" position. There are three colors in the chain with a fourth color for the background. Figure XII-A-1.

A	B	C	D	C	B	A	B	C			C	B
B	A	B	C	B	A	B	C					C
C	B	A	B	A	B	C						
D	C	B	A	B	C	D			D			
C	B	A	B	A	B	C						
B	A	B	C	B	A	B	C					C
A	B	C	D	C	B	A	B	C			C	B

Figure XII-A-1

Each pieced block contains:
   13 squares "A" material
   20 squares "B" material
   12 squares "C" material
   4 squares "D" material
Each plain block is "D" material, and contains:
   4 squares "B" material
   8 squares "C" material
Figures are shown here for a Queen size quilt:
   Size: 7 blocks wide and 9 blocks long
      85.75 plus 2.5 inch borders = 90.75 inches
      110.25 plus 2.5 inch borders = 115.25 inches
      Blocks: Quilt top has 63 blocks with 32 pieced and 31 alternate blocks. There are 49 pieces to the main block. Each block is 12.25 inches square, finished and 12.75 inches square, unfinished.
      Piece: 1.75 inches square finished and 2.25 inches unfinished.
Instructions: See Figures XII-A-2.1, 2.2, 2.3.
      Add leeway to length of strip listed in text.
      Corners will be pieced into alternate blocks. Section III-C.
      Pieced blocks (32):
      Calculate the length of strip to cut: Multiply the length of the side of the unfinished piece by the number of blocks in the quilt to determine the length of strip needed for all blocks. Cut as many strips of each color as there are pieces of that color in one block:
      2.25 × 32 = 72 inches
         Cut 13 strips "A" material (or spot cut 416 pieces).
         Cut 20 strips "B" material.
         Cut 12 strips "C" material.
         Cut 4 strips "D" material.
      Spot cutting of pieces can be done on some material by cutting strips (with or without rotary cutter) and crosscutting individual pieces. The

Plate XII-A.

following photograph shows how this was done with a material in which the flower motifs were staggered. Plate XII-A-1.

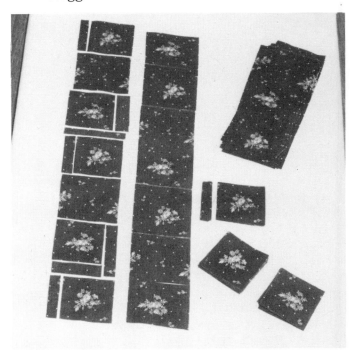

Plate XII-A-1.

EXTENDED TRIPLE IRISH CHAIN II

Queen size 91 x 115 in.

A Color Material

13 strips 2.25 x 74 in. for pieced blocks

scrap

Purchase 2 3/8 yards A color material.

B Color Material

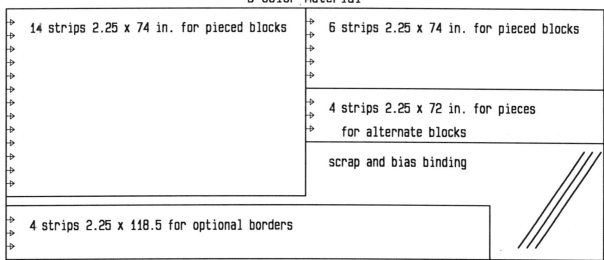

14 strips 2.25 x 74 in. for pieced blocks

6 strips 2.25 x 74 in. for pieced blocks

4 strips 2.25 x 72 in. for pieces
   for alternate blocks

scrap and bias binding

4 strips 2.25 x 118.5 for optional borders

Purchase 4 1/2 yards B color material.

Figure XII-A-2.1

EXTENDED TRIPLE IRISH CHAIN II

Queen size 91 x 115 in.

C Color Material

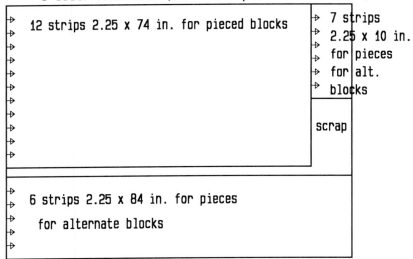

12 strips 2.25 x 74 in. for pieced blocks

10 strips 2.25 x 44.25 in.
for pieces for
alternate blocks

2 strips 2.25 x 74 in. pieces for alt. blocks

scrap

4 strips 2.25 x 118.5 in. for borders

Purchase 3 5/8 yards C color material.

C Color Material (alternate plan - no borders)

12 strips 2.25 x 74 in. for pieced blocks

7 strips
2.25 x 10 in.
for pieces
for alt.
blocks

scrap

6 strips 2.25 x 84 in. for pieces
for alternate blocks

Purchase 2 5/8 yards C color material.

Figure XII-A-2.2

EXTENDED TRIPLE IRISH CHAIN II

Queen Size 91 x 115 in.

D COLOR MATERIAL

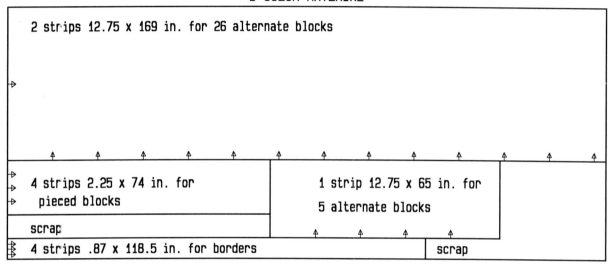

2 strips 12.75 x 169 in. for 26 alternate blocks

4 strips 2.25 x 74 in. for
pieced blocks

1 strip 12.75 x 65 in. for
5 alternate blocks

scrap

4 strips .87 x 118.5 in. for borders

scrap

Purchase 5 1/8 yards D color material.

D COLOR MATERIAL - plan 2 with backing included

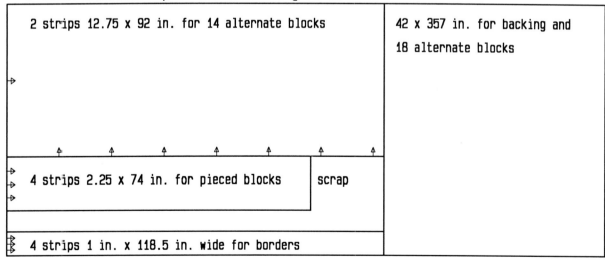

2 strips 12.75 x 92 in. for 14 alternate blocks

42 x 357 in. for backing and
18 alternate blocks

4 strips 2.25 x 74 in. for pieced blocks

scrap

4 strips 1 in. x 118.5 in. wide for borders

Purchase 13 1/2 yards D color material.

Figure XII-A-2.3

Alternate blocks (31): "D" material
Cut 31 - 12.75 inch squares.

Note: Backing may be "D" material also. In this instance, side panels on two lengths of backing can be used for part of alternate blocks (9 blocks each, or 18). Three yards of "D" material would be sufficient for the top. Figure XII-A-2.3 - Plan 2).

Pieces for corners:

2.25 × 31 = 69.75 inches
Cut 4 strips "B" material.
Cut 8 strips "C" material, **or, preferably** adjust length of strip to material available.

Cut 2 strips 2.5 by 72 inches and 10 strips 2.25 by 42.75 inches.

Construct quilt as directed in Sections III and IV. If one piece is spot cut, as in example shown, construct each row of strips less that one piece and any other isolated pieces in one or two sections, and then add in the special piece after the cross cutting is done, as illustrated in Plate XII-A-2.

Plate XII-A-2

Row 1: BCDCB. Row 2: BCB. Row 3: CB and BC. On Rows 2 and 3, and 5 and 6 there will also be another piece which will have to be added in separately.

Borders: Allow 118.5 inches.

The second border (example) was made from "C" material. However, in other colors, it might be appropriate to make the second border in "B" material which is already available. Follow alternate cutting layout plan for "C" color material (a saving of one yard of material) if you choose to make the second border of "B" color material.

Binding: "B" material.

Backing: Purchase 10.5 yards of material (3 lengths).

Plan 2. Saving of material is effected if backing is the same as "D" color material:

Refer to Section IV-E, Figure IV-E-2. Make backing first. Narrow strips for borders may need to be pieced.

Purchase in one piece: 3 yards for top unit and 10.5 yards for backing and remaining alternate blocks, or 13.5 yards. Figure XII-A-2.3.

XIII.
Extended Triple Irish Chain III

A. 49 piece block - 2 color chain
Continuity of chain by sashing method

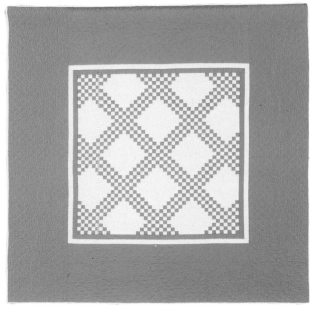

Plate XIII-A.

This elegant example shows how the Irish Chain can be used as a Medallion. The wide borders open for fancy quilting are inspired by the Amish quilts and are of equal importance to the chain pattern.

The sashing and corner system was recommended by the Ruby McKim Studio* and published in the *Kansas City Star*.

The following figure contains 9 blocks only. However, a quilt or wallhanging requires 15 or 25 blocks minimum. A group of nine only will appear as a cross if turned on the diagonal. Figure XIII-A-1.

Note: An 81-piece block and an alternate block with three pieces in each corner would produce the same length chain, but it would have one more piece at the edge all the way around, giving it a more solid appearance.

Each pieced block contains:
    25 squares "A" material
    24 squares "B" material
Each alternate block is plain.

Pieced and alternate blocks are separated by sashing strips and corners, which are pieced to carry out the chain.

Figures are shown here for a wallhanging or small quilt.

101 Patchwork Patterns, Dover Publications, Inc., 1962, p. 26.

Size: Five blocks wide and five blocks long, with sashing between blocks. Center unit is 32.25 inches square plus 12 inch borders = 56 inches square.

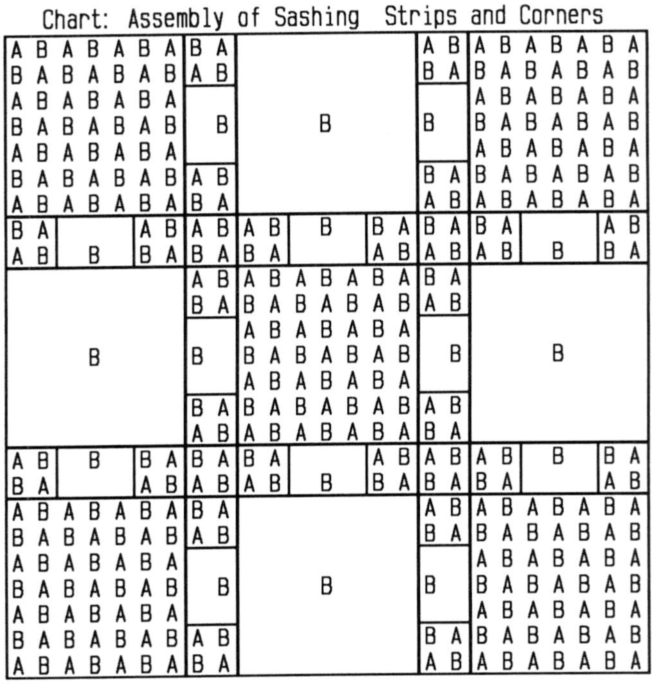

Chart: Assembly of Sashing Strips and Corners

One half of corners are AB and one half are BA.
One half of sashing strip corners are AB and one half are BA.

Figure XIII-A-1

Blocks: Quilt top has 25 blocks, with 13 pieced and 12 alternate blocks. Blocks are 5.25 inches square finished, and 5.75 inches square unfinished.

Piece: Each piece is .75 inch square finished, and 1.25 inches square unfinished.

Sashing: Quilt has 40 sashing strips. Each includes 2 sashing corners. Sashing is 1.5 inches wide finished and 2 inches unfinished.

Corners: Quilt has 16 corners, each 1.5 inches square finished and 2 inches square unfinished.

Instructions: See Figure XIII-A-2.

Continuity of chain by sashing method. Refer to Section III-E.

Pieced blocks:

Figure Rows 1, 3, 5 and 7 as a unit and call it Type I. Figure Rows 2, 4 and 6 as a unit and call it Type II. There will be as many strips as there are pieces in each of these

EXTENDED TRIPLE IRISH CHAIN III

49 Piece Block

Wall hanging 56 in. square

A Color Material

3 strips 1.25 x 53 in. type II	row blocks	
8 strips 1.25 x 36 in. for type I row blocks	strips for corners	binding

4 strips 1.25 x 60 in. for sashing ⌃ corners

4 border sections 12 x 60 in.

Purchase 3 3/4 yards A color material.

B Color Material

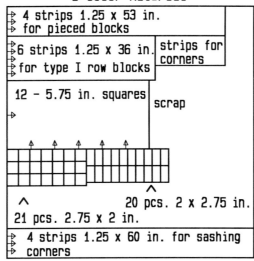

Purchase 2 yards B color material.

Figure XIII-A-2

rows. Multiply the length of piece of each color by the times that type of row is repeated within the block by the number of blocks for the length of strip to cut. (The finished piece is .75 and the cut piece is 1.25 inches.)

Type I Row: A B A B A B A - (4 rows)

1.25 × 4 (Rows 1, 3, 5, 7) = 5 × 13 = 65 inches per strip (add extra leeway for many cuts:

Cut 4 strips of "A" material and 3 strips of "B" material, **or preferably**, cut twice as many strips one-half as long (32.5 to multiple of piece - 33 inches).

Cut 8 strips of "A" material

Cut 6 strips of "B" material

Type II Row: B A B A B A B — (3 rows):

1.25 × 3 (Rows 2, 4, 6) = 3.75 × 13 = 48.75 inches (add leeway)

Cut 4 strips of "B" material.

Cut 3 strips of "A" material.

Follow general instructions, with the difference that strips for all Type I rows are automatically sewn at one time, and likewise strips for all Type II rows are sewn at one time.

Seams may be pressed open if desired. Finger press first, then press with iron, being careful not to slide the iron or stretch the material.

Sashing Strips: (40)

Each sashing strip has one center section of "B" material cut 2.75 inches long and 2 inches wide. Twenty are cut on the long grain and twenty are cut on the crossgrain of the material.

Each sashing strip has 4 pieces "A" and 4 pieces "B" material:

1.25 × 4 = 5 × 40 = 200 inches strip (add leeway)

Cut 200 inches strip of "A" material.

Cut 200 inches strip of "B" material.

One half of this needs to be sewn with the "AB" combination and one half with the "BA" combination. Crosscut, and construct corners and attach to center sections. Keep grain consistent. Do not turn corners sideways.

Vertical sashing: Right hand sashing will be pieced to the right of each pieced block, except the edge block. Left hand sashing will be pieced to the left of each pieced block, except the edge block. Figure XIII-A-3.

Horizontal sashing: One combination will be pieced to the top of the alternate block, and one combination will be pieced to the top of the pieced block, beginning with the second row of blocks. Figure XIII-A-4.

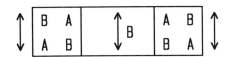

to top of alternate block

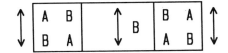

to top of pieced block

Figure XIII-A-4

Plate XIII-A-1 shows the construction of sashing.

Plate XIII-A-1.

Finger press seam allowances. The bowl of a teaspoon is helpful.

Corners (16):

Each corner has 2 pieces "A" and 2 pieces "B" material:

1.25 × 2 = 2.50 × 16 = 40 inches strip (add leeway).

Cut 40 inches "A" material.

Cut 40 inches "B" material.

One-half of this will be sewn with the "AB" combination and one-half with the "BA" combination.

Crosscut, and construct corners. One-half are AB over BA and one half are BA over AB. Do not turn sideways.

Borders: Allow 60 inches.

Binding: "A" color material.

Backing: Purchase 3.75 yards of material.

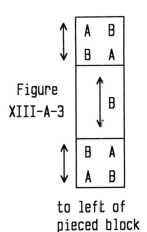

Figure XIII-A-3

to left of pieced block   to right of pieced block

B. 81 piece block - 3 color chain
Continuity of chain by strip method

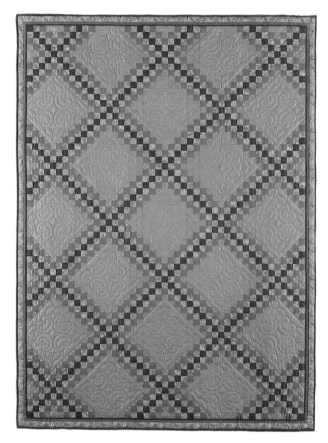

This is a traditional set Triple Irish Chain. Figure XIII-B-1.

A	B	C	D		C	B	A	B	C	D		C	B
B	A	B	C	D	C	B	A	B	C				C
C	B	A	B	C	B	A	B	C					
	C	B	A	B	A	B	C						
D	D	C	B	A	B	C	D	D	D		D		D
	C	B	A	B	A	B	C						
C	B	A	B	C	B	A	B	C					
B	A	B	C	D	C	B	A	B	C				C
A	B	C	D		C	B	A	B	C	D		C	B

Figure XIII-B-1

Each pieced block contains:

17 squares "A" material   20 squares "C" material
28 squares "B" material   16 squares "D" material

Each alternate block contains:

4 squares "B" material   8 squares "C" material

  Figures are shown here for a Twin size quilt:
    Size: 5 blocks wide and 7 blocks long
      56.25 plus 2 inch borders = 60.25 inches
      78.75 plus 2 inch borders = 82.75 inches
      Blocks: Quilt top has 35 blocks with 18 piec-

ed and 17 alternate blocks. Each block is 11.25 inches square finished, and 11.75 inches square unfinished.

  Piece: 1.25 inch square piece finished and 1.75 inch unfinished. Three pieces occurring together will be cut as one piece.

Instructions: See Figure XIII-B-2.

  Add leeway to length of strip listed in text.

  Corners will be set into alternate block by Strip Method. Section III-D.

Pieced Blocks (18):

  Calculate the length of strip to cut: Multiply the length of the side of the unfinished piece by the number of pieced blocks in the quilt to determine the length of strip needed for all blocks. Cut as many strips of each color as there are pieces of that color in one block:

    $1.75 \times 18 = 31.5$ inches

    Cut 17 strips "A" material.
    Cut 28 strips "B" material.
    Cut 20 strips "C" material.
    Cut 4 strips "D" material, **and**
    Cut combined pieces of "D" material, as follows:

  Cut 2 strips of "D" material 4.25 inches wide by 31.5 inches long for top and bottom rows to combine with individual strips for Rows 1 and 9.

Sidestrips:

  Cut 2 strips of "D" material 1.75 by 4.25 inches long for each block for sidestrips. Total of 153 inches.

  Cut 2 strips 1.75 by 76.5 inches. (Cut strips 85 inches long for convenience.)

Alternate Blocks (17):

Cut 17 - 9.25 inch centers of "D" material.

  Corner pieces:

    $1.75 \times 17 = 29.75$ inches.

      Cut 4 strips of "B" material
      Cut 8 strips of "C" material. Save 4 of these strips for sidestrips.

  Top and bottom row:

  Cut 2 - 6.75 by 29.75 inch strips of "D" material.

  Attach BC and CB corner strips to 6.75 inch strips of "D" material before crosscutting.

Sidestrips (Includes 1 piece of "C" at each end):

  Cut 2 strips of "D" material 1.75 by 6.75 inches long for each block. Total of 229.5 inches strip of "D" material needed.

  Cut 3 strips 1.75 by 81 inches long of "D" material (partial strip extra). Cut 34 - 6.75 inch segments.

  Attach corner pieces individually, keeping corners on lengthwise grain.

  Attach sidestrips to center section of alternate block. Attach top and bottom rows.

Borders: Allow 86 inches.

Binding: "A" color material.

Backing: Purchase 5.25 yards.

EXTENDED TRIPLE IRISH CHAIN III

81 Piece Block

Twin Size 60 x 83 in.

A Color Material

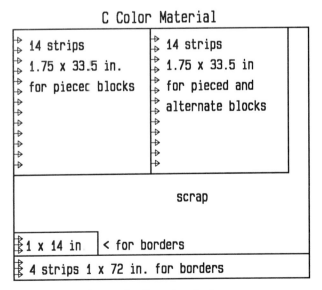

17 strips
1.75 x 33.5 in.
for pieced blocks

bias binding

scrap

.75 x 14 in. < for borders
4 strips .75 x 72 in. for borders

Purchase 2 yards A material.

B Color Material

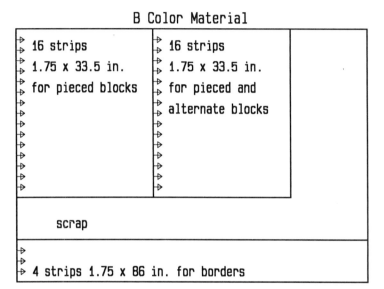

16 strips
1.75 x 33.5 in.
for pieced blocks

16 strips
1.75 x 33.5 in.
for pieced and
alternate blocks

scrap

4 strips 1.75 x 86 in. for borders

Purchase 2 3/4 yards B material.

C Color Material

14 strips
1.75 x 33.5 in.
for pieced blocks

14 strips
1.75 x 33.5 in
for pieced and
alternate blocks

scrap

1 x 14 in < for borders
4 strips 1 x 72 in. for borders

Purchase 2 yards C material.

D Color Material

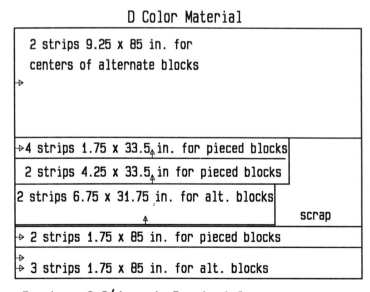

2 strips 9.25 x 85 in. for
centers of alternate blocks

4 strips 1.75 x 33.5 in. for pieced blocks
2 strips 4.25 x 33.5 in for pieced blocks
2 strips 6.75 x 31.75 in. for alt. blocks
scrap
2 strips 1.75 x 85 in. for pieced blocks
3 strips 1.75 x 85 in. for alt. blocks

Purchase 2 3/4 yards D material.

Figure XIII-B-2

XIV.
Extended Triple Irish Chain IV

A. 121 piece block - 3 color chain
Continuity of chain by strip method

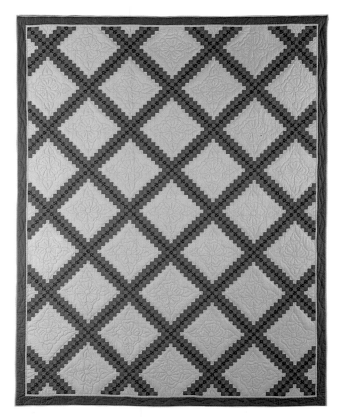

Plate XIV-A.

Cool, analogous colors are employed in this eight point Triple Irish Chain. Figure XIV-A-1.

A	B	C		D		C	B	A	B	C		D		C	B
B	A	B	C		D		C	B	A	B	C				C
C	B	A	B	C	D	C	B	A	B	C					
	C	B	A	B	C	B	A	B	C						
		C	B	A	B	A	B	C							
D	D	D	C	B	A	B	C	D	D	D	D		D		D
		C	B	A	B	A	B	C							
	C	B	A	B	C	B	A	B	C						
C	B	A	B	C	D	C	B	A	B	C					
B	A	B	C		D		C	B	A	B	C				C
A	B	C		D		C	B	A	B	C		D		C	B

Figure XIV-A-1

Each pieced block contains:
21 squares "A" material
36 squares "B" material
28 squares "C" material
36 squares "D" material
Three or five squares of one color occurring together will be cut as one piece.
Each alternate block contains:
4 squares "B" material
8 squares "C" material
Figures are shown here for a Double size quilt:
Size: 7 blocks wide and 9 blocks long
77 plus 3 inch borders = 83 inches
99 plus 3 inch borders = 105 inches
Blocks: Quilt top has 63 blocks with 32 pieced and 31 alternate blocks. Each block is 11 inches square finished, and 11.5 inches square unfinished.
Piece: 1 inch square piece finished and 1.5 inch square piece unfinished. Three pieces together are 1 by 3 inches finished and 1.5 by 3.5 unfinished; five pieces together are 1 by 5 inches finished and 1.5 by 5.5 inches unfinished.
Instructions: See Figures XIV-A-2.1, 2.2.
Add leeway to length of strip listed in text.
Corners will be set into alternate block by Strip Method. Section III-D.
Pieced blocks (32):
Calculate the length of strip to cut: Multiply the length of the side of the unfinished piece by the number of pieced blocks in the quilt to determine the length of strip needed for all blocks. Cut as many strips of each color as there are pieces of that color in one block:
1.5 × 32 = 48 inches
Cut 21 strips "A" material.
Cut 36 strips "B" material.
Cut 28 strips "C" material.
Cut 4 strips "D" material, **and**
Cut combined pieces of "D" material, as follows:
Cut 2 strips of "D" material 5.5 by 48 inches to combine with individual strips for Rows 1 and 11.
Cut 2 strips of "D" material 3.5 by 48 inches to combine with individual strips for Rows 2 and 10.
Sidestrips:
Cut 2 strips of "D" material 1.5 inches wide and 3.5 inches long for each block for the inside sidestrips to the center section (Rows 5 through 7). Total of 224 inches needed. Adjust to available material.
Cut 4 strips 1.5 by 56 inches.
Cut 2 strips of "D" material 1.5 inches wide

and 5.5 inches long for outside sidestrips to the center section (Rows 4 through 8). Total of 352 inches needed. Adjust to available material (increase to multiple of 5.5).

Cut 6 strips 1.5 by 58.7 (60.5) inches.

Alternate block (31):

Center of alternate block:

Cut 31 - 9.5 inch alternate blocks of "D" material.

Corner Pieces:

1.5 × 31 = 46.5 inches

Cut 4 strips of "B" material.

Cut 8 strips of "C" material. Save 4 of these strips for sidestrips.

Top and bottom row:

Cut 2 - 7.5 by 46.5 inch strips of "D" material.

Attach BC and CB corner strips to 7.5 inch strip of "D" material before crosscutting.

Sidestrips:

Sidestrips includes 1 piece of "C" material at each end to complete the corner section. Total of 465 inches strip of "D" material needed.

Cut 13 strips 1.5 by 37.5 inches long of "D" material (partial strip extra). Cut in 7.5 inch segments.

Attach corner pieces individually, keeping corners on lengthwise grain.

Attach sidestrips to center section of alternate block. Attach top and bottom rows.

Borders: Allow 108 inches. Cut 1 - 1 inch border and 1 - 3 inch border, by choice, from the "B" and "C" materials, respectively.

Binding: Purchase separately.

Backing: Purchase 6.5 yards.

EXTENDED TRIPLE IRISH CHAIN   IV

121 Piece Block – 3 Color Chain

Alternate Block by Strip Method

Double size 83 x 105 in.

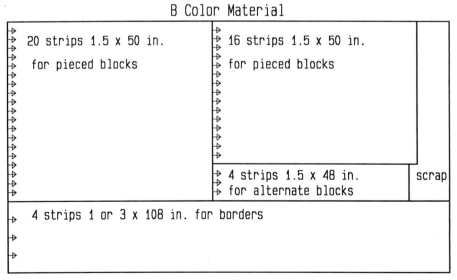

A Color Material

21 strips 1.5 x 50 in. for pieced blocks

scrap

B Color Material

20 strips 1.5 x 50 in. for pieced blocks

16 strips 1.5 x 50 in. for pieced blocks

4 strips 1.5 x 48 in. for alternate blocks

scrap

4 strips 1 or 3 x 108 in. for borders

Purchase 1 3/4 yards A material.   Purchase 3 1/2 yards B material.

Figure XIV-A-2.1

EXTENDED TRIPLE IRISH CHAIN IV

121 Piece Block – 3 Color Chain

Alternate Block by Strip Method

Double size 83 x 105 in.

C Color Material

20 strips 1.5 x 50 in. for pieced blocks	8 strips 1.5 x 50 in. for pieced blocks
	8 strips 1.5 x 49 in. for alternate blocks
	scrap
4 strips 1 or 3 x 108 in. for borders	

Purchase 3 3/8 yards C material.

D Color Material

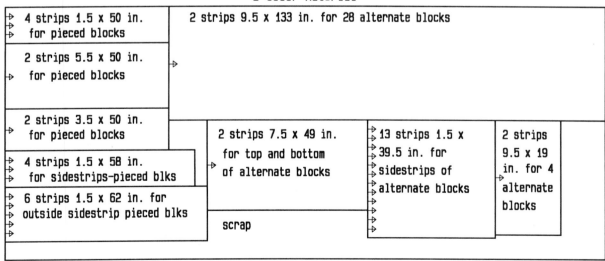

Purchase 5 1/2 yards D material.

Figure XIV-A-2.2

B.   81 Piece Block - 2 or 3 Color Chain
Continuity of Chain by Sashing Method
Reverse Block Set - Alternate Blocks in Corners

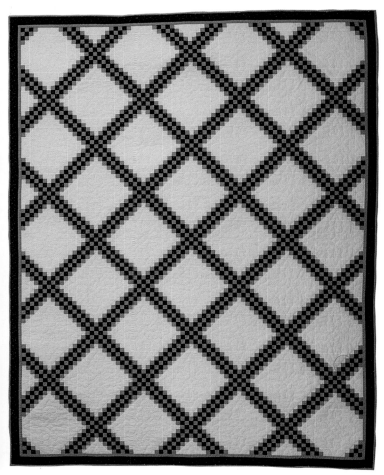

Plate XIV-B.

One advantage of this quilt is that the chain is extended at the edges to produce a good effect in each corner when the block set is reversed. It is a different look in an Irish Chain.

Figure shows a three color chain. Materials "A" and "C" are the same color in this quilt. Figure XIV-B-1.

Note: The same effect can be accomplished by constructing a 121 piece block and adding one row of pieces around the outside edge.

Each pieced block contains:
17 squares "A" material
28 squares "B" material
20 squares "C" material
16 squares "D" material

Three squares of one color occurring together will be cut as one piece.

Each alternate block is plain.

Pieced and alternate blocks are separated by sashing strips and corners, which are pieced to carry out the chain.

Figures are shown here for a Double size quilt:
Size: 7 blocks wide and 9 blocks long
79 plus 2.5 inch borders = 84 inches
101 plus 2.5 inch borders = 106 inches

Blocks: Quilt top has 63 blocks, 31 pieced and 32 alternate blocks. Each block is 9 inches square finished and 9.5 inches unfinished.

Piece: 1 inch finished, 1.5 inches unfinished. Combined pieces: 1.5 by 3.5 inches and 1.5 by 5.5 inches.

Sashing: 2 by 9 inches finished, and 2.5 by 9.5 inches unfinished.

Corners: 4 inches square finished, and 4.5 inches square, unfinished.

Instructions: See Figures XIV-B-2.1, 2.2.
Add leeway to length of strip listed in text.
Pieced Blocks: (31)
Calculate the length of strip to cut: Multiply the length of the side of the unfinished piece by the number of pieced blocks in the quilt to determine the length of strip needed for all blocks. Cut as many strips of each color as there are pieces of that color in one block:
1.5 × 31 = 46.5 inch strip
Cut 37 strips "AC" material.
Cut 28 strips "B" material.
Cut 4 strips "D" material.
Cut 2 strips of "D" material 3.5 by 46.5 inches to combine with individual strips for Rows 1 and 9.
Cut 6 strips 1.5 by 46.5 inches for sidestrips to the center section of three rows.
Cut into 3.5 inch segments (extra strip).

Alternate Blocks (32): "D" material. See Section III-E.
Cut 32 alternate blocks 9.5 inches square.
Corner squares (80) - 40 left and 40 right corner squares: (Note: Four sets of squares must be constructed if there is a nap or one-way print.)
1.5 × 2 = 3 × 80 = 240 inches each color (or 4 strips - 60 inches long).
Cut 4 strips 1.5 by 60 inches of "A" material.
Cut 4 strips 1.5 by 60 inches of "B" material.
(Seams: One half of the seam allowances will

Figure XIV-B-1

EXTENDED TRIPLE IRISH CHAIN IV

81 Piece Block with Sashing

Double Size 84 x 106 in.

AC Color Materials

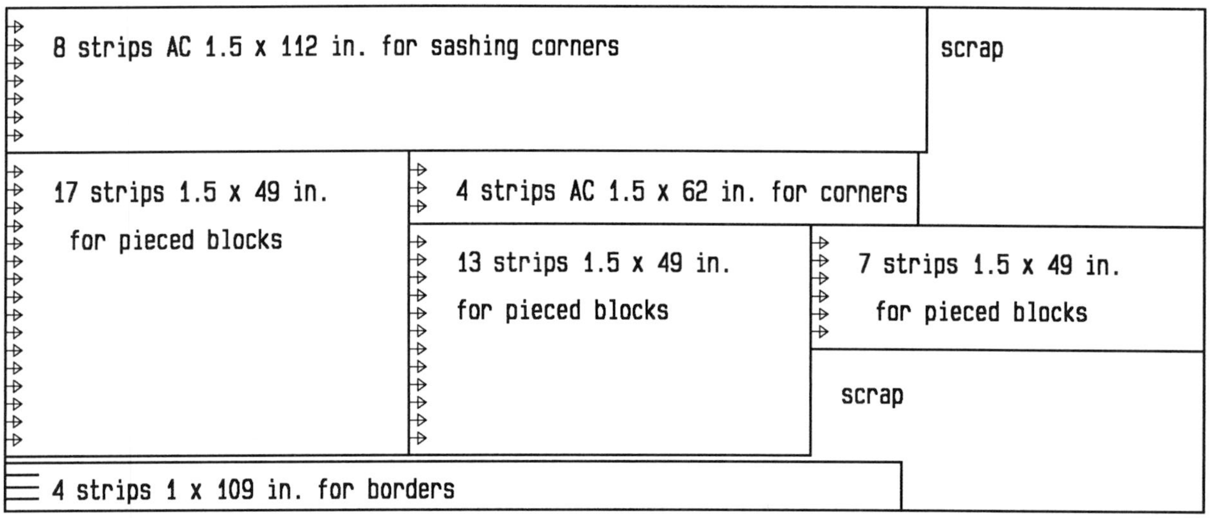

8 strips AC 1.5 x 112 in. for sashing corners

scrap

17 strips 1.5 x 49 in.
   for pieced blocks

4 strips AC 1.5 x 62 in. for corners

13 strips 1.5 x 49 in.
   for pieced blocks

7 strips 1.5 x 49 in.
   for pieced blocks

scrap

4 strips 1 x 109 in. for borders

Purchase 4 1/2 yards AC material.

B Color Material

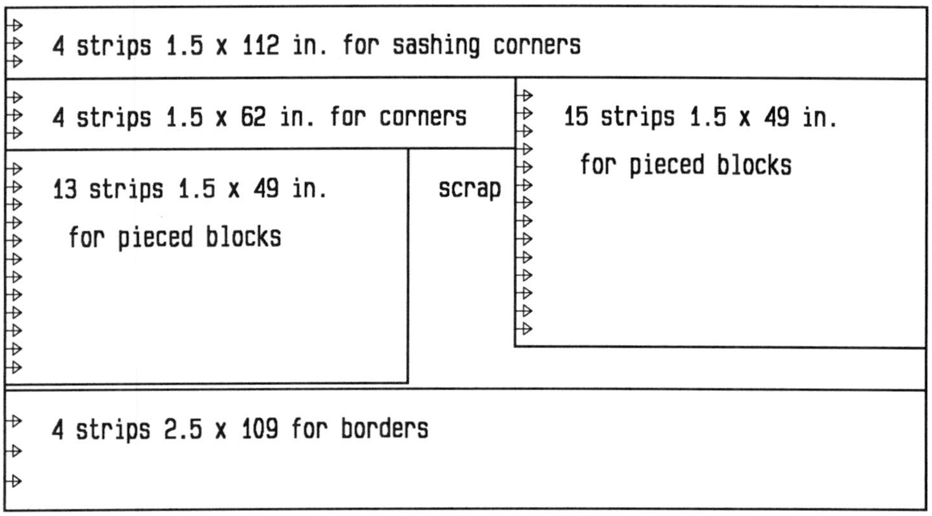

4 strips 1.5 x 112 in. for sashing corners

4 strips 1.5 x 62 in. for corners

15 strips 1.5 x 49 in.
   for pieced blocks

13 strips 1.5 x 49 in.
   for pieced blocks

scrap

4 strips 2.5 x 109 for borders

Purchase 3 1/2 yards B material.

Figure XIV-B-2.1

EXTENDED QUADRUPLE IRISH CHAIN III

121 Piece Block - 4 Color Chain

Twin Size 61 x 83 in.

A Color Material

21 strips
1.5 x 29 in.
for pieced blocks

scrap

Purchase 1 yard A material.

B Color Material

20 strips
1.5 x 29 in.
for pieced blocks

16 strips
1.5 x 29 in.
for pieced blocks

scrap

4 strips 1.5 x 28 in. for alt. blks.

4 strips 2.5 x 87 in. for borders (optional)

Purchase 2 3/4 yards B material (includes borders).
Purchase 2 yards B material (no borders).

C Color Material

20 strips
1.5 x 29 in.
for pieced blocks

8 strips
1.5 x 29 in.
for pieced blocks

8 strips
1.5 x 28 in.
for alt. blocks

scrap

4 strips 2.5 x 87 in. for borders (optional)

Purchase 2 3/4 yards C material (includes borders).
Purchase 2 yards C material (no borders).

D Color Material

20 strips
1.5 x 29 in.
for pieced blocks

12 strips
1.5 x 28 in.
for alt. blocks

binding

4 strips 2.5 x 87 in. for borders (optional)

Purchase 2 3/4 yards D material (includes borders).
Purchase 2 yards D material (no borders).

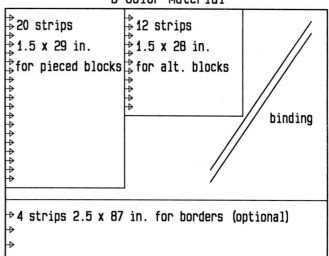

Figure XV-A-2.1

EXTENDED QUADRUPLE IRISH CHAIN III

121 Piece Block – 4 Color Chain

Twin Size 61 x 83 in.

E Color Material

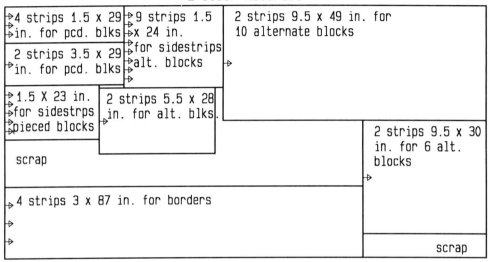

Purchase 3 1/4 yards E color material.

Figure XV-A-2.2

Multiply the amount needed for each block by the number of pieced blocks for the total length needed. Divide by the total number of pieces replaced (6) and increase to the next multiple of 3.5. Cut as many strips as total pieces replaced. (2 × 3.5 = 7 × 18 = 126 ÷ 6 = 21 inches).

 Cut 6 strips 1.5 by 21 inches.
 Cut into 3.5 inch segments.
Alternate blocks (17): Figure XV-A-3.

Center of alternate block:
 Cut 17 - 9.5 inch alternate blocks of "E" material.
Corner pieces of alternate block:
 1.5 × 17 = 25.5.
  Cut 4 strips of "B" material.
  Cut 8 strips of "C" material.
  Cut 12 strips of "D" material.
  Cut 2 strips of "E" material 5.5 by 25.5 inches to combine with individual strips for top and bottom.
  Attach "BCD" and "DCB" strips before crosscutting.
Sidestrips:
 Full sidestrip includes one piece of "D" and one piece of "C" material at each end, to complete the corner section. Total strip needed - 187 inches.
 Cut 9 strips 1.5 by 22 inches. Cut into 5.5 inch segments.
  Attach "C" and "D" pieces or "D" and "C" pieces to each end, keeping pieces on the lengthwise grain.
  Attach sidestrip to center section of alternate block.
  Attach top and bottom rows.
Borders: Allow 86 inches.
Binding: "D" material, or purchase separately.
Backing: Purchase 5¼ yards.

Figure XV-A-3

XVI.
Creative Variation

A. Irish Ribbons

The Ribbons Pattern, though complicated in appearance, is relatively easy to make. Figure XVI-A-1.

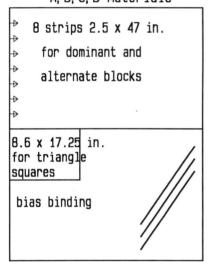

Figure XVI-A-1

Each main block contains:
　8 squares each of "A" and "B" materials
　4 squares each of "C" and "D" materials
　8 squares of "E" material (background)
　4 triangle squares, one each of "A," "B," "C"
and "D" materials, each with a yellow half.
Each alternate block contains:
　4 squares each of "C" and "D" material
　24 squares of "E" material (background), **or
preferably**, 2 - 6.5 inch squares (the equivalent of
9 squares each), plus 6 squares.
　4 triangle squares, one each of "A," "B," "C,"
and "D" materials, each with a yellow half.
All strips will be cut the same length for convenience
(even though alternate blocks require 2.5 inches less in
length); therefore, totals can be made for the cutting
layout chart of the pieces in the dominant and alternate
blocks.
　There are 8 pieces of each of the four colors (32) in
each set of 1 main-1 alternate block.
　There are 32 pieces of the background color in each
set of 1 main-1 alternate block, as shown in the example.
However, the best way to plan the alternate block would
be to consolidate the two sets of 9 pieces each, leaving
6 individual pieces only. The consolidated pieces would
be 6.5 inches square.
　There are two each of the four colors of triangle
squares (8) in each set of 1 dominant-1 alternate block.

Figures are shown here for a Twin size quilt:
　Size: 5 blocks wide and 7 blocks long
　　60 plus 2.5 inch borders = 65 inches
　　84 plus 2.5 inch borders = 89 inches.
　Blocks: Quilt has 35 blocks with 18 dominant and
17 alternate blocks. Each block is 12 inches square finished and 12.5 inches square unfinished.

Piece: 2 inches square finished, and 2.5 inches square
unfinished.
　Instructions: See Figure XVI-A-2.

IRISH RIBBONS

Twin Size 65 x 89 in.

A, B, C, D Materials

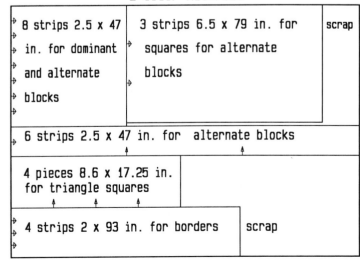

Purchase 1 5/8 yards each of
A, B, C, and D color materials.

Purchase 4 3/8 yards E color material.

Figure XVI-A-2

Add leeway to length of strip listed in the text.

Calculation will be made by "Set" of 1 dominant-1 alternate block. There will be one alternate block left over.

Length of strip to be cut is determined by multiplying the length of the side of one unfinished square by the number of sets in which it appears.

Set of 1 dominant-1 alternate block:

2.5 × 18 sets = 45 inches

Cut 8 strips each of "A" and "B" materials.

Cut 8 strips each of "C" and "D" materials.

Cut 14 strips of "E" material (background).

Cut 34 - 6.5 inch squares of "E" material (two for each block).

Two-Triangle Squares: Refer to Section IV-D.

The measure of the side of the square needed to construct the two-triangle square is ⅞ inch longer than the measure of the side of the finished square, to allow for edge and center seams.

Two - 2-triangle squares of each of four colors are needed for each set of 1 dominant-1 alternate block. They require 1 square each of light and dark color material.

Sets: 18 sets require 18 squares each of light and dark color material.

A practical unit of material will be 3 squares by 6 squares, or 8⅝ inches × 17¼ inches. Cut one each of colors "A," "B," "C" and "D," and cut four of color "E," or the background color.

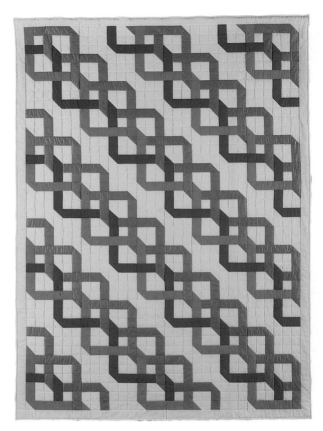

Plate XVI-A.

Begin diagonal line in upper left hand corner of all triangles.

Borders: Cut one border from background material.

Binding: Any one of the four ribbon colors.

Backing: Purchase 5⅝ yards for backing.

Glossary and Symbols

Applique: to lay a piece of material, either geometric or patterned shape, on a background of material and stitch it down.

Carding: A combing process by which fibers are organized in preparation for spinning and weaving.

Component: a part of the whole. A type of geometric quilt block is composed of equal divisions, commonly called pieces, as a 9-piece, a 25-piece, a 49-piece, making a grid. Each division (piece) may be divided into two or four units, for which the word "component" is a convenient term.

Dominant color: the color which has the most significance to the pattern.

Dominant block: the block which carries the greater part of the pattern.

Hypotenuse: the side of a right angle triangle that is opposite the right angle.

Isosceles: having two equal sides (triangle).

Nap: a word for distinguishing the qualities of the lengthwise grain of a textile material that make it the same from one direction only (not reversible). It may have a nap in weaving, as corduroy, or be considered to have a nap in pattern, as a one-way print.

Pieced: pieces of uniform shape sewn together to form a unit of a textile work, or the whole of a textile work, commonly a quilt.

Right angle triangle: a triangle with one 90 degree angle.

Right angle isosceles triangle: a triangle with one 90 degree angle and two equal sides.

Sashing: strips of material used to separate quilt blocks.

Seampoint: the point at which two seams meet, commonly one-eighth to one-fourth inch (or seam allowance) from each edge, in piecework.

Segment: a length of strip which is the same as 3 (or more) finished pieces, plus seam allowance.

Strata: the seaming together of successive strips of material, to be cut apart and resewn to comprise quilt blocks. The word "strata" in this context was first used by Barbara Johannah.

Stripping: building a block, or partially building a block by adding strips from center outward.

Up-end: determining the "top" of a material with a nap or one-way print and keeping the top away from you on the layout table and sewing machine.

$\times$: a figure to show "times" in multiplication.

$\div$: a figure to show "divide by" in division.

Graphics and Photo Index

Plates

Single Irish Chain

Extended Single Irish Chain

Double Irish Chain I

Extended Double Irish Chain II

Triple Irish Chain I

Extended Triple Irish Chain II

Extended Triple Irish Chain III

Extended Triple Irish Chain IV

Extended Quadruple Irish Chain III

Creative Variation

Irish Chain Quilts
Bibliography

Bentley, Diane. "Make It Patchwork." *The New Era*. pp. 18-21, February, 1978. Utah: The Church of Jesus Christ of Latter-Day Saints. (Quilts from Springville Utah Museum of Art.)

Bishop, Robert and Safanda, Elizabeth. *A Gallery of Amish Quilts*. pp. 68-69. New York: E.P. Dutton & Co., Inc., 1976.

Bold and Beautiful Quilts, No. 3778, p. 12. Kansas City, MO: Martha's Studio, Inc.

Brackman, Barbara, "The Quilts at Children's Mercy Hospital." *Quilter's Journal*. No. 25 pp. 12-13, 1984.

Colby, Averil. *Quilting*. New York: Charles Scribner's Sons, 1971.

Colonial Homes. p. 58, March-April, 1981.

Country Living. p. 60, February, 1983.

Cox, Warren Earle. "Design." *Encyclopedia Britannica*. Vol. 7, pp. 259-260, copyright U.S.A., 1956.

Freeman, Jean Todd, "American Heritage: Pieced Patchwork." *Woman's Day*. pp. 66-69. July, 1972.

Grandmother's Authentic Early American Patchwork Quilts, Book No. 23, p. 5. St. Louis, MO: W.L.M. Clark, Inc., 1932.

Hagood, Carol Cook. "A Shamrock Quilt and Pillows." *Decorating and Craft Ideas*. p. 54-55, March, 1982.

Hardy, A.C. "Colour." *Encyclopedia Britannica*. Vol. 6, pp. 52-60, copyright U.S.A., 1956.

Hatch, Betsy. "Color Theory for Quilters." *American Quilter*. pp. 39-41, Summer, 1985.

_____. "Color Theory for Quilters." *American Quilter*. pp. 51-52, Fall, 1985.

_____. "Color Theory for Quilters." *American Quilter*. pp. 43-49, Winter, 1985.

Johannah, Barbara. *The Quick Quiltmaking Handbook*. Menlo Park, CA: Pride of the Forest Press, 1979.

Johnson, Orinne. *The Farmer's Wife Magazine, Quilts, New Patterns and Designs*. p.1, St. Paul, MN, 1937. (rep. Barbara Bannister, Alanson MI, 1982.)

Lady's Circle Patchwork Quilts, p. 21, Issue 22, 1981.

_____, p. 11, Winter, 1982.

Lemon, Bonnie. "Color in Quilts." *Quilter's Newsletter Magazine*. pp. 8-9, June, 1977.

McKim, Ruby. *101 Patchwork Patterns*. New York: Dover Publications, Inc., 1962.

"Mrs. Herbert Hoover's Colonial Quilt." (Ruby's Quilting Party). *Quilt World*. pp. 11-15, December, 1976.

Old Time Quilts. FC-155. p. 13, New York: Farm and Fireside. (Part Pamphlet - no date).

Quilts, Book 190, H-9002 C-32. p. 16, The Spool Cotton Co., 1942.

Tennison, Sarah Beth. "Letter to Editor." *Quilter's Newsletter Magazine*. p. 32, May, 1979.

"The Great American Quilt Classics, Irish Chain." *Quilter's Newsletter Magazine*. pp. 16-19, March, 1979.

Thompson, Shirley. *The Finishing Touch*. Edmonds, WA: Powell Publications, 1980.

Tribuno, Bertha Reth, Comp. and Ed. *Heritage Quilting Designs*, from the collection of Dorathy Franson, Cedar Rapids, IA, 1981.

Wilder, Rose Lane. *Woman's Day Book of American Needlework*. New York: Fawcett Publications, Inc., 1961.

Other Books Published By AQS

Original Quilting Designs by Loraine Neff. . . . . $ 7.95

America's Pictorial Quilts by Caron Mosey $19.95

Award Winning Applique Technique by Carolyn and Wilma Johnson $17.95

Thimbles and Accessories, Antique and Collectible by Averil Mathis $19.95

Missouri Heritage Quilts by Bettina Havig $14.95

Quilt Art Annual Engagement Calendar by AQS . . . . $ 8.95

Texas Quilts, Texas Treasures by Texas Heritage Quilt Society $24.95

Somewhere In Between: Quilts and Quilters of Illinois by Rita Barrow Barber $14.95

Scarlet Ribbons, American Indian Technique For Today's Quilters by Helen Kelley $15.95

Dear Helen, Can You Tell Me? . . . all about quilting designs by Helen Squire $12.95

Sets & Borders by Gwen Marston & Joe Cunningham $14.95

The Grand Finale by Linda Denner $14.95

American Beauties: Rose & Tulip Quilts by Gwen Marston & Joe Cunningham $14.95

Collecting Quilts: Investments in America's Heritage by Cathy Florence $19.95

Add $1.00 additional for postage & handling.

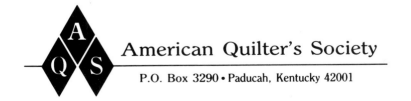

American Quilter's Society

P.O. Box 3290 • Paducah, Kentucky 42001